"In *The Feel Rich Project*, *Psychology Today* blogger and CFP® Michael Kay goes beyond the run-of-the-mill, nuts-and-bolts manuals for personal finance. With a focus on values, strategies, and helpful worksheets targeting insight and change, Kay offers a valuable guide to help readers move from money misery to living richly."

—BRADLEY T. KLONTZ, Psy.D., CFP® co-founder of the Financial Psychology Institute ™, associate professor in Financial Psychology & Behavioral Finance at Creighton University Heider College of Business, and co-author of *Mind Over Money: Overcoming the Money Disorders That Threaten our Financial Health*

"Michael Kay gently and expertly guides his readers from Money Misery to Money Mastery. Michael's work is packed with insight, practical tools, and personal stories that will help the well-to-do and the want-to-do-better to achieve clarity and confidence about their finances and their relationships."

—MARK BRYAN, co-author of *Money Drunk/Money Sober* and *The Artist's Way at Work: Riding the Dragon*

THE

Feel Rich
Project

Reinventing Your
Understanding of True Wealth to
Find True Happiness

Michael F. Kay, CFP®

THE FEEL RICH PROJECT
Edited by Jodi L. Brandon
Typeset by Kristin Goble/PerfecType
Cover design by Howard Grossman/12E Design
Printed in the U.S.A.

To order this title, please call toll-free 1-800-CAREER-1 (NJ and Canada: 201-848-0310) to order using VISA or MasterCard, or for further information on books from Career Press.

The Career Press, Inc.
12 Parish Drive
Wayne, NJ 07470
www.careerpress.com

Library of Congress Cataloging-in-Publication Data

Names: Kay, Michael F., author.
Title: The feel rich project : reinventing your understanding of true wealth to find true happiness / Michael F. Kay.
Description: Wayne, NJ : Career Press, 2016. | Includes index.
Identifiers: LCCN 2016010608 (print) | LCCN 2016017462 (ebook) | ISBN 9781632650498 (paperback) | ISBN 9781632659491 (ebook)
Subjects: LCSH: Money--Psychological aspects. | Wealth. | Finance, Personal. | Happiness. | BISAC: BUSINESS & ECONOMICS / Personal Finance / General. | SELF-HELP / Personal Growth / Happiness.
Classification: LCC HG222.3 .K39 2016 (print) | LCC HG222.3 (ebook) | DDC
332.024/01--dc23
LC record available at https://lccn.loc.gov/2016010608

DEDICATION

To my love, college sweetheart, wife, Wendy, who has walked this journey with me through the laughter and the tears since 1973. And to my wonderful and caring children and their mates, Elyssa and Dave, Mitchel and Rachel—thank you for the love, laughter, and unending support. You all keep my values clear and focused.

ACKNOWLEDGMENTS

Huge thanks to Rochelle Moulton who pushed, cajoled, and prodded me to completion—even when I resisted. Her vision for this work was crystal clear even when mine was cloudy. Sydney LeBlanc for her guidance, help, and a multitude of stories: fascinating, funny, and heart-breaking. Christina Guthrie, who worked so hard and diligently helping me through the final edits. And the team at Career Press, including Lauren Manoy and Jodi Brandon, for bringing my work to fruition. Lastly, to my "family" at Financial Life Focus, for putting up with me during the times I went missing.

CONTENTS

Introduction

There are hundreds of how-to personal finance books on the shelves—books that promise to make you a better investor, help you pick winning stocks, make you rich, make you successful, help you retire at 40. You name it, there's a book that will tell you "how to." Nice, right?

The premise of those books is simple: The writer knows a secret that no one else knows, and for a mere pittance, the secret will be revealed to you without so much as having to burn one stick of incense.

Well, I hate to break it to you, but other than some nuts and bolts information that you might never have learned or have forgotten, there are no secrets! What does "feeling" rich have to do with actually "being" rich? In fact, our beliefs and feelings have everything to do with the results.

Mary, a single woman in her 60s, was raised by parents who grew up during the Depression; her parents were great savers, but never felt they had enough. Mary's money experience told her that nothing was more important than savings. Spending was a painful proposition. When Mary came to see me, she had accumulated well in excess of $7 million. When I broached the idea of her putting her money to some enjoyable means, she rejected the idea—not because she didn't want to, but because she was afraid she didn't have enough. Mary didn't feel rich, even though her resources far exceeded her needs.

Carol, 47, grew up with parents who lived a pretty extravagant lifestyle and showed her the finer things in life. Unfortunately, Carol and her husband were bigger spenders than earners, and soon found themselves drowning in debt. Carol believed she was rich and felt rich—and couldn't reconcile the fact that their financial ship was sinking fast.

There are hundreds of examples of people holding onto beliefs that steered their actions to create disharmony and dysfunction in their lives. In too many cases there is a misalignment of beliefs and reality. Too many folks hold onto messages that do not serve their happiness, security, or life goals. In fact, millions of people are living in money misery, being hounded by debt collectors and wondering how they're going to pull themselves out of what seems like an unsolvable problem. Many (not all) of these problems have their genesis in their beliefs and behaviors.

If you look around, you can probably spot many examples of people who are financially secure, and who don't wear their wealth on their backs or live paycheck to paycheck. They place high value on family, education, experiences, and peace of mind, and they place little or no value on showing the world or their neighbors how financially secure they are. There are many who hold the real riches of the world in their hearts. The love they share with their partners, children, family, and friends is all the riches they need—somehow, a 70-inch curved panoramic 3-D flat-screen TV doesn't move the needle for them.

One of the greatest challenges of our world is that we are swimming against a very powerful tide. When I grew up, television consisted of seven channels, and of course commercials were the fuel that drove that engine. We even had to get up to change the channels. (Imagine that!) Today we are bombarded by hundreds of channels and the Internet, which has insidiously figured out how to place ads everywhere. Movies, videos, reality TV, magazines, podcasts, blogs, not to mention e-mails, prompt you to buy the newest, most popular goods that draw a direct link between your mind's image of how you see yourself or how you wish to be seen and your credit card.

Carl sat back in his chair, pulled out his flip phone, and placed it on the table before our meeting began. I looked at this relic of the '90s a bit bewildered. He saw the look on my face. "It works and it's all I need." He was neither defensive nor apologetic—just completely comfortable with who he was and what he cared about. Carl, with his six grandchildren and close-knit family, considers himself rich. He feels rich because he has that which he values most.

As a society, we are force-fed the idea that our wants must be satisfied in order to be "in"—to be perceived as someone successful and relevant. Big data—those companies that collect information about you, how you shop, where you shop, what you buy, when you buy, what you're likely to buy next, and to what stimulus you respond most—is geared up to prompt your spending decisions. It's a war, carefully waged, to blur the lines between your wants and your needs.

I want you to feel rich, and I believe you can. It is realistic and attainable, as I have seen countless times, but it will not happen overnight or without effort. The process begins with coming to terms with the fact that something isn't working the way you want. You might be living with dread of the monthly credit card bill or phone calls from collections companies. You might be looking into the faces of your young children and wondering how the heck you're going to pay for college. You might be in your mid-50s and see retirement as an impossibility. Whatever your specific thoughts or dissatisfaction around your money life, you want something better.

Together, we will walk through the steps to creating a more satisfying and secure picture of your life. We will establish some baseline information, and you will, with my guidance, craft your reasons for making a change. This is not a miracle, seven-day weight-loss scheme or overnight, get-rich-quick scam; this is about your awareness, your values, and creating the small positive steps to making a real difference.

Let's break down what it takes to improve your financial satisfaction:

1. Basic financial knowledge.
2. Understanding your money mindset.
3. Defining your values.
4. Developing strategies.
5. Putting energy behind the strategies to create action.
6. Making adjustments when necessary and appropriate.

This is not a "how to create your own financial plan" book. It is a "why am I doing this to myself and why I need to make changes" book. In other words, in order to create a path to financial satisfaction that will raise your level of confidence and comfort, there are some steps that you need to take. We are talking about the absence of inertia that *must* be replaced by action. After all, what's the good of a road map, a journey, an action if you're not going anywhere? Throughout this book, you will read a lot of action verbs and exhortations to move from inaction to big, bold, beautiful action.

I want you to actively identify the riches in your life and why they are important to you. Only through that understanding can you begin to see that "rich" is not the newest gadget, latest fashion, or other tangible thing that provides a momentary endorphin rush. The objective of this book is to help you look at money differently and help put you on the road to not only greater satisfaction but also a revised definition of "rich."

The journey will begin with some basic information and data. You will gather and review your current financial information and will refer back to this information throughout the book.

Once you have established some of your money truths, you will explore topics such as money misery and money fantasy. There will be a discussion on your thinking about money and where it came from. We're talking your money history and how it impacts your money mindset now.

Next will be an exploration of values and what I call your *musts*. You will embark on a visioning exercise to help focus your thoughts.

The purpose of reading any how-to book is to gain knowledge and understanding about a topic. The point of this work is to help you understand what's not working and why, and perhaps replace it with a new set of beliefs that will support you in your quest to improve your financial life and your life in general. After all, an improved financial life has implications far beyond the balance in your retirement account.

Lastly, I will provide you with some resources to help you continue to push your happiness and success further. Financial success, like surgery, is not a do-it-yourself program. But you can certainly be so well prepared that your work with a financial professional will be much simpler and much less daunting.

What can you expect while reading this book? Good question; I'm glad you asked. I will ask you some tough, probing and thought-provoking questions, and I expect you will take the time to answer them thoroughly. Some might require time to think and marinate on the topic; others should be simple, top-of-mind answers. I will share stories to illustrate the ideas and hopefully they will resonate with you. I will present you with some exercises that will require you to ponder, consider, imagine, and memorialize your responses. These are designed to be interesting and enlightening.

What won't you get from reading this book? I am not going to teach you why you need disability insurance and how much life insurance you need. I am not going to toss out catchy rules of thumb for you to latch onto. I am not going to review the IRS Code on Passive Activity losses, nor will I tell you your optimal asset allocation. The goal here is to understand your money life now, where it came from, and where you *really* need it to go and why. Technical knowledge is available, and I will help you find it, but the point here is to build your money fitness by dealing with your money mindset. After all, isn't it your mindset that tells you to what you "need" to buy, what you deserve, and that an emergency fund isn't as important as that upcoming vacation? Our money mindset is our mental regulator that either supports our goals or justifies maxing out the credit cards.

Keep in mind that I am not a psychologist, psychiatrist, or therapist. As a Certified Financial Planner Professional™ and Financial Life Planner, I have been working with clients for more than 30 years. While everyone's situation is technically different, it is safe to say that where problems, roadblocks, and troubles exist, one's money mindset is very often at the root. My extensive experience in Financial Life Planning asking questions and listening deeply to clients has furnished me with a wealth of understanding and experience. My intent is to share my experience with you during our time together by offering you the opportunity to do some of the work similar to what my clients and I do one-on-one. The stories I share throughout the book are meant to be illustrative. Each conclusion or action is individual and therefore, you should not read them as "your" solution. It is unethical to offer specific financial advice to readers without knowing the specifics of their financial situation; therefore, I will avoid giving financial advice as much as possible. Instead, I want you to walk away from this experience with that *a-ha!* feeling of self-revelation and knowledge that will prepare you to tackle the nuts and bolts of your own financial needs.

I hope that, as you read and work through the exercises that with each succeeding page, your attachment to the ideas of feeling rich and being rich become real. As you take back ownership and control of your financial life from the button pushers, you will, hopefully, experience a new sense of success, satisfaction, and happiness. A note of caution: Make sure that before you begin each exercise, you have the time, space, and focus to devote fully to thinking through and considering each question. When you finish each worksheet, give yourself a round of applause for your efforts. Each strong effort is a building block toward your success.

So, do a few toe touches and get ready to explore you and some of your *whys*. It's a great place to begin.

Ab Intra

CHAPTER 1

Beginning Your Journey to Overcome Money Misery

Money misery is a condition suffered by too many people in our society. Though I am certain there is no insurance code for this diagnosis, there probably should be. It can come from our internal beliefs, behaviors, and habits, or can be supported from external sources. Money misery can best be defined as feeling frustrated, angry, dissatisfied, confused, or generally lacking in comfort or security around money issues. Not having enough money left over at the end of your paycheck; being burdened by debt that never seems to end; and feeling less successful than your friend, neighbor, colleague, or family member are just a few examples of money misery. In other words, whatever makes you feel insecure, insolvent, or in a cycle of financial constraints is ripe for money misery. You might say, you know it when you feel it.

We are treated every day to "news" of the rich and famous—their opulent lifestyles and the rarified air they breathe. The 1-percenters live an existence that most of us can't even *hope* to experience. Yet their antics and possessions are everywhere for our consumption.

These dramatic differences can make us feel like there is a deep separation between "us" and "them." And it seems that being "them" is way better than being "us." If that doesn't lead us right into money misery, I don't know what does.

Let's be 100-percent clear: Our money misery does not appear out of thin air. We are either taught that possessions equal satisfaction, or we come to that decision by viewing the world around us and seeing ourselves as lacking. Our desire for success leads us to a neverending loop of want. "He who dies with the most toys wins" is a worthy mantra.

Money misery comes from how we interpret what we see versus who we are—you know, what we consider "normal." Our idea of normal comes from the messages we learned growing up. Your parents may have grown up poor or wealthy or in another country—and their experiences became their reality. Those experiences formed their belief system about correct thinking and action, which they more than likely passed on to you. After all, through a child's eye, why would you question what appeared normal?

My grandparents came to this country without money, security, or a job. They figured out how to survive and scraped by with only meager resources. My grandmother would move from apartment building to apartment building during the Depression—wherever she could find a month or two of free rent. That made the difference between starving and surviving.

So of course my father grew up with these lessons firmly implanted in his psyche. His normal was to save, save, save. Never hire someone to do something for you if you could figure out how to do it yourself. His frugality was taken to extremes: His internal "drivers" had him on high ladders, scraping shingles and painting the house, into his 70s. It was stupid to everyone else; to him, there simply was no other option. His money misery came in the form of never feeling comfortable with his resources, because you never know when the next Depression will wipe out everyone.

Money misery has other faces. Measuring yourself against your friends, neighbors, and relatives buys you a ticket into a life of constant competition for first place. There is no comfort in second place—only angst, anxiety, and misery. Overspending and taking on debt out of misplaced guilt is a terrible companion through life. "But I only wanted my kids to have it better than I did!" is just passing on misery to the next generation.

Can we agree that there is more than sufficient money misery around us? Extreme and highly visible wealth possessed by the few stands as a symbol of what everyone wants, which creates a cycle of dissatisfaction and misery. Living as "less than" is not living; it is an existence of pain.

Fortunately, there is a path out. It's not a 12-step program. ("Hi, I'm Carol and I live in money misery.") But The Feel Rich Project *is* about understanding that your beliefs around money and values, in most cases, stem from your childhood and how you see yourself in the world. They set you up for the rest of your life. Without thoughtful, insightful action, you are primed to listen to the shadowy voice that whispers "I want," "I deserve," "I need" in order to feel good. You turn to retail therapy to pacify the feeling of not having enough, which invariably turns into yet more misery. The cycle continues.

Some examples: the home-buying spree that led to the real estate bubble bursting and a deep, painful recession. Maybe you bought more house than you could truly afford. Or you tapped into your equity to fund vacations or an over-the-top remodel.

Or maybe you got mired in credit card debt and are walking the razor's edge of financial insolvency. All it takes is one life surprise—you lose your job, your spouse loses theirs, you welcome a new addition to the family, there's an unexpected death or divorce—for you to tumble into bankruptcy.

So what's the solution?

First, understand that financial happiness is *not* a function of how much money you make. There are many people who earn a modest income, live within their means, and have extremely high levels of satisfaction. There are also many people who earn piles of money and are miserable. The idea is to identify the *whys* of your feelings around money, and move in the direction of what alleviates pain and increases real satisfaction.

Start by separating your money reality from your money fantasy. The rest of this chapter will be devoted to several worksheets designed to gather both quantitative (numbers) and qualitative (feelings) information. The purpose is to help you separate your money reality from fantasy. Your numbers are your numbers, and your feelings are yours. The point is to promote your knowledge and understanding. For example, a young couple asked us to help with their planning by reviewing their situation. What we found was a net worth statement in the red caused by a ton of student loans. They both earned a modest income, as they are beginning their careers. Their cash flow, which you will have the opportunity to create later in the chapter, was pretty much at breakeven—meaning they are paying their bills but have very little left over. Their question to us was, "Can we afford to buy a house?" Our job was to explain that buying a house was impossible without a substantial increase in earnings or a miraculous windfall that would pay off their school loans. The fact that they are thinking of buying a home tells us that we need to help them separate their fantasy from their reality.

Distinguishing Your Money Reality From Your Money Fantasy

Fantasy lives in your head. It's a nice place to visit, but a lousy place to live your financial life. Our view of reality can be skewed by our experiences. Remember: **Just because you believe something, doesn't make it so.** For example, if you believe "Money is the key to happiness" or "Money is the root of all evil," you might want to consider those beliefs by asking yourself why you hold those beliefs. This isn't about right or wrong; it's about whether your beliefs support your values. What we want to get to is objective reality; you know the facts.

The following worksheet will help you to capture some of your core beliefs about money. Use the information gained in this worksheet to begin to see and understand your core money beliefs and areas that either support you or create dissatisfaction in your life.

WORKSHEET 1-1: REALITY OR FANTASY?

Capture your core money beliefs by asking yourself some questions and recording your answers. Quick reminder: These answers are yours; they are private, honest, and real. Ask yourself whether your answers are being tainted with guilt, shame, or some other factor that makes you feel bad.

- What do you believe about success? *Examples: "I believe success is best displayed by the possessions I own." "I believe success is about paying my bills and putting money away for the future."*

- What do you believe about people who are wealthy? *Examples: "Wealthy people are selfish." "Wealthy people work harder than those who are not."*

- What do you believe about people who are poor? *Examples: "Poor people are satisfied being poor." "Poor people just don't work hard."*

- Is there anyone in your life with whom you feel money competition? Why?

- What makes you worry?

- What provides peace and security?

- What lessons did you learn about money from your mother and your father?

- Was there ever a time when money was not a problem? Why was it not? What made it that way? What did you do differently then that made a difference?

Write down your beliefs, and "tag" them to an example in your life *and* their source.

Here's an example:

I believe: that money should be used to show my success.

Example: I bought that new BMW so everyone knows I'm doing really well at work.

Source: My dad always said we needed to look better than Uncle Jim's family no matter what.

As you work through this, mark your beliefs that are affirming and positive with a star. And note those that create problems or strife in your life with an X.

Ready?

1. I believe:

Example:

Source:

2. I believe:

Example:

Source:

3. I believe:

Example:

Source:

4. I believe:

Example:

Source:

5. I believe:

Example:

Source:

6. I believe:

Example:

Source:

7. I believe:

Example:

Source:

8. I believe:

Example:

Source:

9. I believe:

Example:

Source:

Do have more stars or Xs? Do your money beliefs support the life you want, or have they created a foundation of money misery? The idea is to identify those positives and appreciate them as the strengths you possess. It's what we build on. It is fair to say that for many of us, we tend to underplay our successes and focus on our problems or faults. I'd like to turn that equation upside down. Let's begin with a deep appreciation for our successes, what we've learned, how we've grown, and where we are. Spend some time considering those positives and try to move them up in the order of attention. Now for those damned Xs. The fact is, no one is perfect; no one is free of strife, problems, or weaknesses—it is that which makes us oh-so-very human. Those weaknesses are where we want to begin to improve by gaining knowledge, competence, and mastery little by little.

Did you learn anything new about your money beliefs? Now let's add in some more reality.

Sticking With the Facts

There are certain truths surrounding money that sometimes get washed away, especially if you're prone to justifying what you *wish* to be true. Following are some of those truths:

- **Your income is your income.** It's typically controlled by factors other than your desire. Winning the lottery, marrying into wealth, or running the table in Las Vegas should not

be factored into your income accumulation
strategy.

- **Your expenses can be fixed or discretionary,
  controllable or variable.** It is your job to set
  the boundaries on what is realistic in view
  of your income, your goals, and your ability
  to survive unexpected challenges, like losing
  your job or disability.

- **Your money problems rarely, if ever, solve
  themselves.** Your debt doesn't go away
  because you wish it to (at least without
  bankruptcy, which is a whole other bag of
  problems).

- **Money—and managing your cash flow—is
  active, not passive.** You'll need to take an
  active role in managing your money life.
  Blindly handing over responsibility to anyone else or putting it on the "to do later" pile
  are sure roads to disaster.

- **You can't afford not to get educated about
  and comfortable with your money**. We're not
  talking PhD-level here. You don't need to
  know everything. You just have to get comfortable with the basics and know when and
  where to seek out advice. You can't afford
  not to make educated decisions.

So what are *your* money facts? It's time for the
moment of truth when you can see—all in one place—
your reality.

Your next task is to get a snapshot of your current cash flow and net worth. You may not be excited about these next worksheets, but if we're going to take this journey together, this dose of reality is 100-percent mandatory. If you want to figure out where you're going, it's best to start by knowing where you are.

A note before you start: This might feel awful, especially if you're stuck in a less-than-positive position. You might have to take some time to gather the numbers and documents, but it's here where you need to be spot on with accuracy. But trust me: We'll get through this. Start with information, honesty, and courage; you are where you are, right? So get to it. It's the beginning of a very important journey.

WORKSHEET 1-2: YOUR MONEY FACTS (PART 1)

Use this worksheet to assess where you are financially right now: assets, debts, the whole truth.

Net Worth

	Owner	Value
Assets		
Checking and Savings Accounts		
Checking Account		$
Checking Account		$
Savings Account		$
Money Market Account		$

Brokerage and Investment Accounts (current market value)		
Individual Account		$
Individual Account		$
Joint Account		$
Retirement Accounts (current market value)		
IRA		$
IRA Rollover		$
Roth IRA		$
403(b)		$
401(k)		$
Tax Deferred Accounts (current market value)		
Annuity		$
529 College Savings Plan		$
Real Estate (current market value)		
Primary Residence		$
Vacation Residence		$
Commercial Real Estate		$
Other Assets		
Business (See note 1.)		$

Limited Partnerships		$
Trusts		$
Total Assets		$
Liabilities (current balances owed)		
Primary Mortgage		$
Secondary Mortgage		$
Home Equity Loan		$
Car Loan		$
Student Loans		$
Credit Card Debt		$
Business Loans		$
Total Liabilities		$
NET WORTH (Total Assets – Total Liabilities)		$

Note 1: Business Value: If you own a business, is it saleable?
For example, if you are an independent contractor, you
are considered a business, but it might or might not have
a value to anyone else. If there is no way to measure value,
be very judicious in what number you put down. It's better
to be conservative.

WORKSHEET 1-3: YOUR MONEY FACTS (PART 2)

Detailed Cash Flow

	Monthly	Annually
INCOME		
Salary	$	$
Bonus	$	$
Self-Employment	$	$
Dividend	$	$
Capital Gains	$	$
Royalties	$	$
Pension	$	$
Rental Income	$	$
Social Security	$	$
Other	$	$
TOTAL INCOME	$	$
EXPENSES		
	Monthly	Annually
Housing Expenses		
Property Taxes	$	$
Homeowners' Insurance	$	$
Association/Condo Fees	$	$
Home Improvements/ Maintenance	$	$

Furnishings	$	$
Cleaning Service	$	$
Lawn Maintenance	$	$
Snow Removal	$	$
Other	$	$
Housing Total	$	$
Utilities		
Heat Gas/Oil/Electric	$	$
Water/Sewer	$	$
Garbage	$	$
Cable/Internet/Phone	$	$
Alarm/Security	$	$
Other	$	$
Utilities Total	$	$
Transportation		
Auto Insurance	$	$
Gas	$	$
Maintenance	$	$
Parking/Tolls/E-ZPass	$	$
License Fees	$	$
Public Transportation	$	$
Other	$	$
Transportation Total	$	$
Medical—Out of Pocket	$	$
Medical	$	$

Dental	$	$
Vision	$	$
Prescriptions	$	$
Other	$	$
Medical Total	$	$
Insurance Premiums	$	$
Health Insurance	$	$
Dental Insurance	$	$
Life Insurance	$	$
Umbrella/Excess Liability	$	$
Disability Insurance	$	$
Long-Term Care	$	$
Other	$	$
Insurance Total	$	$
Personal Care		
Groceries	$	$
Hair/Salon	$	$
Gym	$	$
Clothing	$	$
Dry Cleaning	$	$
Pet Care	$	$
Other	$	$
Personal Care Total	$	$
Entertainment		
Restaurants	$	$

Movies/Theater/Museums/Events	$	$
Hobbies	$	$
Vacation/Travel	$	$
Club/Membership Dues	$	$
Gifts	$	$
Charity	$	$
Other (Please list.)	$	$
Entertainment Total	$	$
Other		
Cash/ATM Withdrawals	$	$
Childcare or Eldercare Expenses	$	$
Tuition	$	$
Home Office/Business Expenses	$	$
Alimony Payments	$	$
Child Support Payments	$	$
Miscellaneous	$	$
Other Total	$	$
Liability Payments		
Mortgage (Principal and Interest)	$	$
Auto Loan/Lease Payments	$	$
Student Loans	$	$
Home Equity	$	$
Credit Cards	$	$

Liability Payments Total	$	$
Estimated Tax Payments		
Federal	$	$
State	$	$
Self-Employment	$	$
FICA	$	$
Medicare	$	$
Other	$	$
Tax Payments Total	$	$
TOTAL EXPENSES AND TAXES	$	$
CASH FLOW SURPLUS/ DEFICIT (Total Income – Total Expenses and Taxes)	$	$

WORKSHEET 1-4: YOUR MONEY FACTS (PART 3)

Let's extract some observations from worksheets 1-2 and 1-3 and see what there is to learn from the numbers.

My cash flow is:

_____ Positive (more income is coming in than going out).

_____ Negative (more is going out than coming in).

My discretionary spending is:

_____ Under control (i.e., you have positive cash flow and are saving regularly).

_____ Out of control (i.e., you are spending to the extent of your income or creating debt as a result of your outflow).

My debt situation:

____ Is very manageable.

____ Is somewhat manageable.

____ Gives me night terrors.

My income is:

____ Secure and fixed.

____ Insecure and fixed.

____ Secure and variable. (Variable income might be a result of being self-employed.)

____ Insecure and variable.

I have a good handle on where the money goes each month.

____ For sure

____ Uh ... nope

I save regularly.

____ Yes, I do!

____ I save, just not regularly.

____ Can't seem to do it on my income.

My net worth is: (This is pretty subjective. If you believe you should have $1 million by the time you reach your 30th birthday, you might not feel good about your net worth, but take a shot at how you *feel* about how you are building security.)

_____ Satisfactory for my situation.

_____ Fair, could be better.

_____ Let's put it this way, it's not positive.

What percentage of your income is spent on debt other than mortgage?

_____ 0

_____ 5–10%

_____ 11–20%

_____ More than 20%

What percentage of your income is spent on mortgage debt?

_____ 0

_____ 1–10%

_____ 11–25%

_____ 26–35%

_____ 36–50%

_____ More than 50%

Based on my numbers: (Remember: This is a solo assessment, so try to keep your thoughts about anyone else's situation out of it. Your feeling is important, and you will only muddy the waters if you compare yourself to your imagination of your brother's, neighbor's, colleague's, or friend's financial situation.)

_____ I feel pretty darn good.

_____ I am moderately satisfied.

_____ Help! I need to turn this ship around.

Over the next chapters we will explore more fully these concepts and ideas. I want you to have a baseline of quantitative information on your numbers and qualitative data about how you feel about those numbers to begin to work toward improving the areas that add to your life's satisfaction.

Using the Knowledge and Information You've Gained

What you have here now is a quantitative _and_ qualitative understanding of your money. The numbers are vitally important, but without understanding where your messages, beliefs, and behaviors come from, you are rowing with one oar. You may want forward progress, but trust me: You'll be going around in a circle.

Your history and belief structure can create the bedrock of sanity and satisfaction or a wickedly unstable foundation that will crumble (typically with you still inside).

You want to look at yourself and how you can make changes—even small ones—to replace broken ideas with strong successful ones. It is not an overnight solution, nor will your transition be flawless. There will be bumps. There will be mistakes. But in the end, you can bring yourself a sense of peace and satisfaction. Just stick with the process I show you in this book to take one step at a time. I'll be right here with you.

Preparing Yourself to Transform Money Misery Into Satisfaction

Crossing over from money misery to satisfaction can be a minefield. You need to be prepared to not only do your work, but to jump four possible barricades:

- **Misery is your "normal."** Think about what you do in your daily routine without giving it a thought: whether you put your left shoe on before your right, the hand in which you hold your toothbrush. You do what you do because it has become your "normal." If you spend first and think second, it is because you've become conditioned to do so. Buying on impulse, deferring savings and avoiding tightening your financial belt is following the most comfortable path of existence. What you're really doing is deferring pain. You know intellectually that you'll have to deal with this issue at some point. The question is: How far down the road can you kick that can? You may be deluded by magical thinking—hoping you'll fill-in-the-blank: win the lottery, receive a big inheritance, find a bag of money, or get an inside stock tip (acting upon which *is* illegal).

- **Judgment of your peers sucks.** The fear of being judged by others is a killer (more on this in Chapter 2). It impacts your life from the moment you first start learning to be self-conscious about the reactions of those around you. It guides what you eat and drink, the clothes you wear, and just about every aspect of your thinking. It becomes all about fitting in with your community, your peers, and your family. It's about that primal part of the brain that needs to dominate or control the environment. And though that might have been really important in caveman days, but when you're searching for peace and satisfaction today? Not so much.

- **You defer making tradeoffs.** Until your situation is dire, it's human nature to do nothing. You can't feel future pain, so deferral seems like the best idea. After all, no one likes pain (unless you swing that way, in which case, I'm not judging). Pain avoidance is a big seller in our society. Think of it as self-medicating on overconsumption. But it's a deferral technique that inevitably brings an even bigger pain bill when avoidance no longer works.

- **Your financial literacy is lacking.** Financial literacy is a huge problem. Our schools don't have the time or resources to teach it, most parents don't have the knowledge or the interest, and the financial services industry is a mishmash that can do more harm than good. But there are oases of hope and help. Organizations like the the National Association of Personal Financial Advisors (NAPFA), the Financial Planning Association (FPA), the National Endowment for Financial Education (NEFE), 360 Degrees of Financial Literacy, and the Institute of Financial Literacy have resources to help build a path to a different, more rational, and more satisfying reality.

Transforming money misery into life satisfaction is a journey—not only of financial improvement, but also of self-discovery and awareness. Have you ever experienced a time when you asked yourself, "Why do I think that way?" or "Why do I act that way?" or "Why do I make the decisions I do?" These questions require a degree of courage to ask, and more so, to answer with real awareness. It isn't especially difficult once you transcend the wall of fear that surrounds you and keeps you from peering into difficult corners. What beliefs might you kick over by uncovering some knowledge?

The reality is, you are not to blame for what you learned, observed, and adopted as normal in your upbringing. But you are responsible if you allow broken beliefs and behaviors to continue once you become aware. Because with that awareness comes the responsibility to adopt better habits and teach valuable lessons to future generations. You have a choice whether you want the cycle of money misery to continue in your life and into that of your children.

CHAPTER 2

The "F" Word

If you are squeamish or very proper, no worries about where we're going with this. The four-letter word I want to talk with you about is *fear*. Yes, my friend, fear. It's a close companion in many situations, invited or not.

Fear can be a good thing, offering a layer of protection from some unknown possible future event. It's what you might term "rational fear." Fear of skin cancer leading to the frequent application of sunscreen and periodic visits to the dermatologist makes perfect sense. However, fear can also be an insurmountable irrational wall that keeps you apart from your true desires. Think the girl/boy you were afraid to call in high school, the job you didn't apply for, the dream you dismissed as fanciful.

What beliefs keep us locked in place, unwilling or unable to rub too closely to the walls of our comfort zone? For some, a fear of failure, fear of judgment, fear of rejection, or just the endless loop of beliefs that we are not up to the task keeps us locked in place.

There is a way past the fear, a way past the limiting beliefs to something more satisfying and real. It begins with excavating the root of these self-imposed limitations. It does take a level of courage to break the pattern of behavior to break through that wall of comfort. Hey, what's the worst-case scenario? When it comes to a broken or unsatisfying money life, do you have anything to lose except the misery?

I stood at the edge of the zip line platform, looking at the strand of wire that extended over a ravine to a platform several football fields away. My heart was pounding into my temples, my mouth was dry, and sweat was pouring off me. Was I really going to strap a harness on myself and clip it to a pencil-thin metal cable and leap off? There was no part of my consciousness that felt this was rational. But then I thought to myself, "If not now, when?" I watched fearless children fly across the void, laughing loudly. Some even clipped in "Superman" style (aka belly down). I admit I was horrified. But I asked myself, "Would all these parents send their progeny soaring across a canyon if they didn't think it was completely safe?" Maybe they knew something I didn't. Oh yes, I knew fear. But I did it anyway.

The fear gamut runs from spiders to social workers; from stepping on a crack to being in a room without a light. Most of it is irrational—except for the spiders, of course—but that doesn't make fear any less intimidating. (Think of irrational fear as a belief that is tethered to something powerful that you have taken as truth.)

When it comes to your money life, fear plays a prominent role in your behaviors and beliefs. Here are two big ones: the *fear of outliving your resources* and the *fear of being perceived as unsuccessful.*

Figuring Out the Source of Your Fear

There are tons of books and studies on fear: fear of success, fear of failure and the various demons that prevent your forward progress, and books that offer paths to more productive possibilities. *Big Magic: Creative Living Beyond Fear* by Elizabeth Gilbert, *Rising Strong* by Brené Brown, and *Fear: Essential Wisdom for Getting Through the Storm* by Thich Naht Hahn, are just a few.

In order to get your financial life in order, you need a clear understanding of what obstacles exist for *you* and from where they originated. We know that your money fears often stem from how you were imprinted with the idea of money when you were young. Here's the thing: Everyone has a money imprint—what you believe about money today that you carried with you from your earliest experiences. Understanding your money imprint will position you to focus on messages that don't serve you well today. Use Worksheet 2-1 to take a look at your earliest associations with money, so that you can better understand not only your core beliefs but also how they developed.

WORKSHEET 2-1: YOUR MONEY IMPRINT

1. What is your earliest memory of money? (What do you remember hearing or experiencing about money?)

2. As a child, what was the most important lesson you learned about money? (Examples: *"If you got it, flaunt it." "Save for a rainy day."*)

3. Growing up in your family, how was money used? Was it to reward, punish, survive, impress, control, help others, have fun, buy love, reach goals, or something else?

4. What are the one-sentence messages about money that have stuck with you from your childhood? Where did you hear these messages?

5. When you were young, did you consider your family to be rich, poor, or somewhere in between—or was it not present in your consciousness?

6. What were you taught about money when you were growing up and by whom?

7. What were the spending/savings patterns of your mother? Your father?

8. In your family, was money a source of conflict? A tool for achieving goals?

9. Are there any "a-ha!" moments as you review your responses? Write them here.

Remember: What you believe becomes your idea of normal. If you grew up believing that it is important to save for a rainy day, then that is the action that will feel right, normal, and proper. Anything that deviates from that will feel unnatural and wrong. It's your normal.

If you grew up with money as the source of arguments, then the mere mention of money can cause that sick, queasy feeling in your stomach. It brings you back to your early memories of screaming matches over money. It's your normal. Can you connect the dots between your past and your present?

So how do you separate your "normal" that supports your success from the unsupportive or downright destructive?

Is Your Fear Your Friend or Your Foe?

"Friendly" fear is pretty darned rational and one that can spur you to make good, meaningful, and forward-thinking decisions. Think fear associated with being dependent on your children for survival. That friendly fear leads to a habit of savings, keeping expenses in check, and being mindful of the consequences of not acting in your own best interest. If you lived through times when resources were scarce, you probably have created a money mindset that safeguards against a reoccurrence. If you use the fear of outliving your resources as a significant driver in your belief system, you'll save money. You'll invest it, protect it, and make spending decisions in the context of your "fear factor." The idea of outliving your resources is so discomforting that planning and preparing become as natural as breathing.

But the unfriendly version can do exactly the opposite: It can drive decisions that ensure painful outcomes. Fear becomes the enemy when things such as fear of others' judgment or fear of being perceived as unsuccessful drives your spending decisions. In my early career, I was a practicing CPA, and besides working for a firm, I was moonlighting doing tax returns for extra money. I was referred to someone who asked me to come to their home to do their taxes. I pulled up to this magnificent home in a gorgeous neighborhood. Walking up the front steps, I was prepared to enter this lavish abode, feeling very good about my luck to acquire this wealthy new client. I was greeted at the door and brought into a virtually empty house, with lawn furniture in the living room and folding chairs around an aluminum table. During the conversation, I discovered that while this couple was "thrilled" to be living in this amazing home, they were drowning in debt and could barely make ends meet. This was an example of a poor financial decision made by the desire to be perceived as successful. Their money misery was further aggravated by the large tax bill due. It was not a happy experience for anyone.

If you fear being perceived poorly by your friends, family, and community, you'll make decisions that channel your money into things that scream "success": the car you drive, the house you buy (or rent), the clothes you wear, and so forth. Fear that you can't keep up with your peers, colleagues, relatives, or neighbors will lead to a desperation that can only lead to failure. A perfect example landed in our office in the form of someone who lived in a very expensive area and had very successful friends. In order to "keep up," he stopped paying his estimated taxes and then stopped filing returns, knowing he had spent the tax. He was caught in a downward spiral from which he couldn't extricate himself. He was too proud to admit he was not in the same financial league as his friends, so he kept up the cycle of tax evasion—until . . . let's just say, the outcome was not positive for anyone. He had more fear of the perception of others than the fear of being caught by the IRS. Needless to say, his money mindset came from somewhere, and it did not support either his success or a peaceful night's sleep.

We know there are negative money messages and positive ones. The negative ones are easy, and it usually begins with a lack—lack of sound financial knowledge and lack of self-esteem.

And yet sometimes, you can take a positive money mindset in a direction that becomes negative. Let's say you have a fear of outliving your resources. If you become a rational saver, you enhance your chances of having a comfortable retirement. But if you take that money message to an extreme and become miserly, your life quickly spins out of balance. Why would anyone sacrifice their life to the extreme so that when they are older, they can feel more comfortable? When fear turns something positive—saving for the future—into a manic inability to enjoy some of the bounty in the present, misery ensues.

Your experiences growing up have been built into your thoughts, beliefs, and behaviors—and ultimately developed into your money mindset. It is your normal. And if your normal has created chaos, unhappiness, and financial misery, then it might be time to examine it, test it, and work toward changes that bring you true happiness.

Getting Control Over Your Fear

While you can't alter or erase your experiences, you can remodel and reshape the behaviors that came from those experiences. You can create a new mindset that affirms your success. It's a matter of defining your pain threshold. Does continuing your current beliefs and behaviors create more pain than the challenge of making changes?

Think about the cycle of someone who employs the concept of retail therapy as a result of some stress, anxiety, or disappointment:

They have a "need" to buy something to make them feel better about themselves.

They succumb to the need, even though they know that they will have to find the money to pay for it—eventually.

The purchase is made—the credit card is hit.

A moment of satisfaction—the itch has been scratched.

The credit card comes in—misery and worry follow close behind.

They buy something else to take their mind off the worry.

This cycle continues: Credit cards get maxed out, bill collectors call, and the overspender buys more. The hole just gets deeper. Something has to give. The misery cycle continues.

But there are great ideas, paths, and money messages to support you and move you out of the pattern of fear-based failure to something much more satisfying. Let me help. Here are some favorable money messages that can work *for you* to build a successful financial life:

Pay yourself first.

Save for a rainy day.

Money is used to provide security.

Money is used to help those less fortunate.

Don't buy anything that you cannot afford to pay for.

Waste not, want not.

A penny saved is a penny earned.

Money cannot buy happiness.

Money doesn't grow on trees.

Money provides options and opportunity

And here are some that tend to work *against you* when building financial security:

Money is the root of all evil.

Never let anyone think you don't have money.

He who dies with the most toys wins.

You can always make more money.

You can never have enough money.

Without money you are nothing.

God will provide.

If you've got it, flaunt it.

Lack of money means lack of friends.

Life is a game, and money is how you keep score.

See how these beliefs can skew your actions and attitudes? Positive money messages are affirming and supportive, and help maintain a compass point that puts life and money in a more balanced perspective.

Athough it is vital to face up to your financial reality, it is not necessary, helpful, or healthy to do so while carrying around the fear and guilt associated with that burden. This emotional overload can blind you to the fact that there is always a solution. It can debilitate your ability to find clarity and move to a better place.

Laboring under debt can feel like a very real, physical burden. I have watched people walk into my office literally loaded down with debt, like Marley's ghost, dragging heavy chains wherever they go. You can see it in their defeated demeanor.

Change is challenging. But remaining in the same situation is tougher. So here's your next assignment: You have the *proven* ability to make changes in your life when they've needed to be made. Use Worksheet 2-2 to tap into those experiences, which can serve as fuel for your Feel Rich Project.

I want you to begin to excavate experiences that were successful as a model of what is possible. As you work through these questions, think about what fears you have overcome and what obstacles you worked through in your journey. It doesn't matter if the experience was from 40 years ago or last week; find a success that was yours.

|||||||||||

WORKSHEET 2-2: YOUR TRACK RECORD

Think back to a time when either money was not a problem *or* you successfully made a change (not necessarily regarding money). Have it firmly in mind? Now answer a few questions about that experience.

1.　How did you make the change?

2.　How did you feel when the obstacle was overcome?

3.　What habits did you put in place that made change possible?

4.　What did you believe about yourself as a result of your success?

5. What you believe becomes your reality. What did
    you learn you are capable of?

Wow, great work! Understanding your money imprint—
and how it plays out in your life—is *huge*. We all have
fears and we all have overcome challenges. The question
is whether you can see how your fears work for or against
you, and where they work to your detriment, how you
can substitute another reality—a better reality—to create a much more satisfying outcome.

In the next chapter we'll explore how you define
happiness, and the role your values and the people in
your life play in getting you there.

CHAPTER 3

Happiness Is Personal and So Are Your Values

There are books and articles galore on happiness and values: Gretchen Rubin's *The Happiness Project,* Sonja Lyubomirsky's *The How of Happiness,* Dan Harris's *10% Happier,* Jessica Virne's *Happiness Lessons from the Dalai Lama,* Hyrum W. Smith's *What Matters Most: The Power of Living Your Values,* and Marc Allen Schelske's *Discovering Your Authentic Core Values,* just to name a few. These resources approach the topic from myriad angles and ideas—all worthy efforts to help point you in a direction toward the positive aspects of a life that's filled with challenges and obstacles.

The gist of all these books on happiness is pretty much the same, though: Our happiness is found through intentionally and with awareness living those values that money cannot buy. We know what happiness is when we feel it; the challenge is creating an intentional path focused on what we value. The idea is that intentional path is created with, as Stephen Covey says, the end in mind. Think of it as an "if/then" mindset. **If** I do this, **then** I get that. If your end in mind is built on what you care most about—your values—then the decisions to be made become clearer and more focused. For example, if I wish to protect my family financially, in case I die before I finish accumulating, then I need to buy life insurance. The idea of a premature death doesn't sound happy, but making sure my family is protected is aligned with my values.

Happiness can either be a Pop Rocks experience that arrives with a bang and dissipates into nothing, or it can be sustaining and long lived, like the feeling of watching your happy children at play or mastering a valued skill. For many people, buying something new provides a certain good feeling; they might call it happy. But if the result of the purchase places them in financial jeopardy or further away from what they care most about, then the happiness fades away really quickly. The thrill is gone, replaced by something much less satisfying.

Achieving a life filled with happiness isn't easy, but it's well worth the effort. Though we could quibble about the idea of happiness, feel free to replace or supplement the word *satisfaction* or other word that best describes how you feel. In other words, we know there are challenges, problems, and difficult unexpected transitions to overcome, but as long as we are guided by the principles of our values, we can say our happiness level is pretty darn high.

This chapter will call on you for some pretty deep thinking and a whole lot of honesty. You might find yourself resisting some of the concepts of the assignments. I want you to find the internal resources to walk with me on this part of the journey. It is the foundation of what we're trying to accomplish together. The ideas are to identify your values, understand your beliefs about your life and your money, and begin to map out a better iteration of the life you want and for which you are willing to create shifts in your thoughts and actions. The goal is your peace of mind fueled by your values, resulting in your happiness. Let's begin.

Thinking About Your Values

Values are the cornerstone of your beliefs. Your values might be centered on your family, your friends, your education, how you treat others, or how you wish to be treated. For example, someone who values their environment will not open the car window and toss out a bag of trash. Someone who values the environment will recycle, conserve resources, reduce their carbon footprint, and be mindful of their actions to best support the well-being of the planet. Someone who values their financial security will make sure they save money actively. They will not consume beyond their ability to sustain a savings plan that makes them feel that they are moving in the right direction. A person who values their health will make sure to act in a way that supports that value: exercise, whole foods, appropriate rest, regular checkups with their physician. The idea is to match the appropriate action with your belief.

Think about what *you* value. (Yes, it's time for you to get out your notebook or blank page on your computer or tablet.) Using the topics that follow as a guide to get you started, think about your values and what they mean to you. Remember to, as Simon Sinek wrote, "start with why":

- Health
- Family
- Financial security
- Accomplishment
- Community
- Spirituality (however you define it)

Note: Make sure you understand the difference between a want and a need in this exercise. We start using "I want" with our first words. Have you ever heard a youngster in the store with their parent? It's often a constant stream of "I want. . . ." Many of us reach adulthood with the same bell clanging in their brains: "I want—I want—I want!" Maybe it's the child part of us that still connects to the idea of "I see—I want." The movies, media, and constant parade of opulence and things rubs up against that part of our brains that craves that "sweet," too. But it isn't a need, and it certainly isn't a value. Needs, on the other hand, must be met; otherwise, we are merely in survival mode. Needs are essential and are therefore valued.

Examining the Connection Between Values and Needs

Are you familiar with Maslow's Hierarchy of Needs? I could devote a chapter explaining Maslow's theory, but instead I will leave it up to you to read more. There are copious sources from Wikipedia to Maslow's book, *Hierarchy of Needs: The Theory of Human Motivation*. Maslow created a pyramid that begins with a base level of *physiological needs* (air and water). It then moves up to *safety,* to *love/belonging*, to *esteem,* and finally to *self-actualization* (the highest point in the progression). The point is, in order for us to grow beyond our current state, we must improve our ability to live closer to our values. In order to move closer, we need to build upon a foundation of appropriately aligned beliefs, behaviors, and habits.

Let me introduce you to Ben. He has more money than he could ever spend in two lifetimes. Yet, he is miserable, is significantly overweight, has had more than one heart-related "event," and sees everyone else's folly who doesn't act as he does. Ben wouldn't spend a dime until he researched every purchase, regardless of how trivial, and then proceeded to try to bargain down the price with the seller, as if it were his last penny. I've experienced this several times and each time, I feel so uneasy that being with him has become excruciating. His feeling around financial security is played out by his behavior. His story is not unlike many I have worked with; losing a parent at a young age created financial stress during his formative years. He will never feel the security that actually exists in his life unless he examines his beliefs and understands his values. The balance of his net worth does not create joy or balance in his life. It's safe to say that Ben has an irrational belief that everyone is out to screw him and that he is smarter than everyone else by his willingness to go toe-to-toe over pennies. What does he value? The coins in his pocket outweigh his health in his hierarchy of his needs—or, at least, his actions seem to indicate just that.

Going Deeper to Determine True Wants and Needs

If we are to believe Abraham Maslow, our values begin in our feeling of safety for our families and ourselves. However, safety is just the second step on the ladder to self-actualization. A deeper dive into our values and beliefs is necessary in order to define what we truly want and need, which rises to high levels of personal development and awareness such as love and belonging and self-esteem. Note: Self-esteem is not derived from possessions, but measured by that inner feeling that comes from living one's values.

Before diving into the next worksheet, take a minute to focus on the connection between these ideas of "needs" with your values. The problem occurs when there is a disconnect between those two concepts, as there will be an obstacle to understand and overcome. For example, someone with low self-esteem might surround themselves with "things" as an outward display of their achievement. Conversely, someone with high levels of self-esteem may have no need to prove anything to anyone. A lack of safety, a lack of love and belonging, along with self-esteem, all provide ample opportunity to create havoc in trying to achieve their true values.

Worksheet 3-1 gives you the opportunity to look at some of these areas and test your beliefs. Ready to get to work? Take all the time you need to complete this worksheet. This is *important*.

WORKSHEET 3-1: HOW ARE YOUR VALUES AND BELIEFS WORKING OUT?

The first step is to set up or copy the template on pages 71–72.

1. First, list your values in the left hand column (for example, your family, your health, your financial security, sense of community, well-being, work, etc.). Don't stop with my examples. Add everything, in the broadest sense, that you value.

2. Now the hard part: What do you believe about each item on your values list? (Note: This self-assessment is big work. It might be something you've never thought about before.)

3. Next, complete your *whys.*

4. Finally, consider whether those beliefs are working for you or against your highest needs (your values).

Use the examples as a starting point. Remember: The objective here is to gain more insight on whether you are clearly focusing on your values, and whether your beliefs and behaviors are in harmony with what you really care most about.

My Values	What Do I Believe About This Value?	Why Do I Believe It?	Is It Working?
Relationship with my family.	*These relationships are key to my happiness and well-being.*	*I have lived through and witnessed the absence of good relationships and the devastation left in its wake.*	*Yes. My relationships with my wife and children are open, comfortable, loving, and close.*
Health			
Financial Security			

My Values	What Do I Believe About This Value?	Why Do I Believe It?	Is It Working?

You see, it's not so difficult. It simply demands your honesty, even if it's painful. Writing painful experiences is important. It takes it out of your head and heart, and puts it in black and white on the page. The difficult parts of life are real. A spoonful of sugar might help the medicine go down, but the reason for the medicine still exists.

Great work. You might need a break after this exercise—time to integrate what you wrote and how you feel about what you learned. Take a walk, go for a run, take a shower, listen to music, do some yoga—whatever will support you after this profound excavation. When you're ready, you can come back to tackle the last exercise in this chapter.

Mapping Out Your New Path

Children have a wonderful ability to enter the world of fantasy, to create a world with their imagination. The world is created, entered, and explored in these tiny wonderful minds. Then we grow up and are taught to keep our feet on the ground and our heads in the present. "Stop *daydreaming!*"

You are now invited to start daydreaming and reenter the world that was thought to be a waste of time and childish. Your willingness to walk this path of your imagination is an important step in your journey to consider other possibilities. Although you won't earn frequent-flyer miles, at least you don't have to stand in line at security, and there are no bags to pack or carry. In fact, the object is to unpack the bags you've been toting around for far too long. But feel free to take your shoes off.

Your assignment is to imagine a life where:

- Your values reside in the forefront of your thoughts and actions.
- Your happiness is derived from living according to those stated values.
- The experiences that created your current situation no longer control your beliefs and behaviors.
- You can rewrite your script to a new reality.

Ask yourself questions like:

- What would my life be if _____ (my health was not a problem, money was not a problem, etc.)?
- Who could I be if _____?
- What could I do if _____?

Once you have pondered these questions, create a mind map of possibilities. What's a mind map, you ask? Glad you asked.

A *mind map* is basically a diagram used to visually organize information. It is usually created around a central concept drawn in the middle of the page with major ideas branching out from there. Each branch is then fleshed out with more and more detail and information pertaining to each new branch.

Mind mapping can be done on the back of an envelope or with readily available software programs. You can stand in front of an easel or white board and draw to your heart's content. The objective is to make it a living and growing document that accounts for information known and unknown and can be added to or modified as your thoughts and knowledge change. Want to give it a try? Begin with your central theme—say, "Feel Rich"—and begin drawing lines to ideas that create a new reality. For example, from your central box, you might draw a line to a bubble that says "Debt-Free." From that bubble, you might create ideas to get you to that state—the to-dos or actions associated with moving toward your goal. The key is getting all your thoughts from your vision to the paper. Make it as detailed as possible and as real as possible.

Another bubble might be "Saving for Retirement." From there you might list, how much, where, why, and so forth. Get to the details.

You might also have bubbles that talk about college savings, saving to buy a house, or funds to help others. You are the artist and you get to use whatever colors you want to make it beautiful and *real*. Your map can be linear, be colorful, use pictures or drawings, or just be boxes and lines. Try to have fun with it and remember: Keep adding as the ideas pop into your mind.

You've done great work. Here are some takeaway thoughts. Your mind map is never finished; it is a constant work-in-progress. You get to refine, alter, and change it as your vision changes and has more clarity.

A word on clarity: Think of a mountain you can see in the distance. It might look like a carpet of green encapsulates the entire landscape. As you get closer, you begin to see that there are patches of open spaces—rocky outcropping among the trees. As you get even closer, you might see the individual trees, trails, and perhaps a small stream spilling over a rock or a few deer noshing on berries. The closer you get, the picture goes from macro to micro.

Magic happens when you get a grand view, from a distance, and then get down into the details as you are able to get closer and closer to the reality. That's what makes this journey so unique: Your viewpoint of where you are, where you came from, what you believe, why you believe it, whether or not it works for your ultimate goals (of safety) and what you need to do to make changes are all there for you to work with and work through.

As you gain clarity, you have a greater ability to ask questions and drill down on issues that rise in order of importance. Your clarity provides you with the opportunity to ask a lot of "what if?" questions. For example, money issues might nudge you toward working with a planner, or family issues might present a need to consult with a psychologist or therapist. You don't need to walk this trail alone; there is help out there to help support you.

|||||||||

Okay, take a break. You've earned it. In Chapter 4 we will sharpen your picture of safety and investigate your "pillow factor." Great work!

CHAPTER 4

What's in Your Bags?

We all have baggage. You know, that stuff we carry around with us that came from past experiences. The "funny" thing is, these experiences are so ingrained in our brains that we don't even notice them. Did you ever have the experience of being with someone new, and they did something so heinously odd that you just had to say something? You know, like eating pastrami on white bread with mayo. It's just not done! Everyone knows that pastrami is eaten on rye with mustard—period! But for the "offending" person requesting two slices of white and a healthy slathering of mayo, they are acting completely normally. It's all how you look at your experiences and beliefs.

There's an old expression that rolls around in my brain from time to time, along with so many other axioms, words of wisdom, and sayings: A watched pot never boils. Of course, this saying is entirely incorrect. The pot *will* boil, provided there's a fire underneath; it's just a matter of enough heat and patience.

We grow up with all sorts of beliefs that have been injected, absorbed, and assimilated into our subconscious. They become a part of our idea of normal, whether or not they are actually correct. Take, for example, this conversation between a couple we'll call Ilene and Eric. Ilene grew up in a family in which money was not especially plentiful, and survival was on the top of the list. Eric grew up in a more affluent family in which money was much more available. When I asked them each to talk about what is important to them in building a financial future, here's what I heard.

|||||||||||

Eric: "I would like to build a reserve fund to provide a safety net for our children. I don't know how to quantify it, but I am afraid that they will not be able to find careers that will afford them a suitable living. My parents were there for me while I found myself. I would like to be able to give them a down payment on a house."

The look in Ilene's eyes bespoke complete disbelief in what she was hearing. Respectfully, she held her tongue until it was her turn to share her thoughts.

Ilene: "I grew up with a completely different set of beliefs. My parents expected that my siblings and I would live a lifestyle that our salaries could afford. I understand a safety net of sorts—such as, if they have difficulty, they could move back home until they could afford their own place. But the idea of supporting a lifestyle that they couldn't sustain on their own doesn't seem to be doing them any favors. Oh, and by the way, your parents didn't give us the down payment; we paid back every nickel."

||||||||||

Without going into the rest of the conversation, this example illustrates how different experiences create different beliefs. Unless we challenge our experiences and ask some very important questions, we will continue under our current beliefs unabated. If our beliefs and habits are destructive, there's a better than even chance that the conclusion will not be pretty.

In this chapter, you will explore what keeps your head off the pillow at night and why, and you will also explore what would allow a good night's sleep without financial worry. You will read a wonderful story called "The Pickle Jar" that illustrates how simple money habits can reflect deep core values. And finally, you will have the opportunity to think about possible small steps to help you begin to move in the direction that would be like that warm cup of chamomile tea before bed—*ahhhhhhh.*

What's Your "Pillow Factor"?

We all have restless nights every once in awhile. Maybe it was that cup of coffee late in the day or that caffeine-packed chocolate brownie for dessert? For those whose mornings arrive as a rescue from a night of uncontrollable worry and stress, recognize that the cause of the sleep-lessness was not food-based. For those who are dogged by bill collectors, threatening letters, or just the knowledge that your financial house is not secure, it is a night of misery that you know will just repeat itself the next night. It's a terrible cycle. All you want is to have a level of comfort with your financial life that puts you more in control. What factors and circumstances have led to your current feeling of unease? What beliefs do you hold that might be in need of a second look?

One way to examine your level of comfort is to measure your comfort level with your financial life. I call it your "pillow factor." In other words, what keeps your head off the pillow at night, or what allows you to sleep peacefully?

We are experts at the irrational. We make decisions based on our beliefs or on what we believe we *should* do, even at the cost of what we know is good sense. There are great resources available that demonstrate this wonderfully: *Sway* by Ori and Rom Brafman, *Predictably Irrational* by Dan Ariely, and *Your Money and Your Brain* by Jason Zweig, to name a few. A richness of great works is available to help you deepen your understanding, and let's face it: Without understanding, you're going exactly nowhere.

Time for a short exercise. Worksheet 4-1 provides a great opportunity to do what is referred to as a "Ben Franklin." Do you know what that means? It's also known as a "T-account." For those of you who ever took a basic accounting course, you know all about T-accounts. For those who have never had the pleasure, in bookkeeping and accounting, a T-account is used to understand the impact of transactions on various types of accounts.

The T-account allows for an understanding of transactions, the plusses and the minuses. Benjamin Franklin used it to help make decisions by recording the pros and cons of a particular issue. Here's an example: Say the issue is whether to spend $5,000 on a vacation. The pros might be you will have time with those you love, you will have fun, you will get a much-needed break from work, being in the sun has certain health benefits, and you get to recharge your batteries to be more creative and effective at work when you get back. The cons: It will put a strain on your budget and leave you in more debt. It will be stressful knowing there will be a bill coming. Okay, there's your T-account. In evaluating a decision, you must weigh the pros and cons against what you value most. What solutions might you come up with? Do you see how this tool could help in considering more objectively challenges that confront you?

Try to do this exercise in one sitting when you have some quiet, uninterrupted time. Don't filter your thoughts; there will be time for that later. Write as quickly and as thoroughly as possible without taking a break. Take a few deep breaths and clear your mind of all the things you need to do. Oh, and *please turn off your cell phone!* (I bet you didn't see *that* coming.) Ready? Go!

WORKSHEET 4-1: WHAT'S YOUR PILLOW FACTOR?

Here's your opportunity to look at the pros and cons of making the sorts of decisions you'll need to change your future.

A couple of suggestions:

1. Frame your decision as a question, such as "Should I buy a new computer?"

2. List the pros and cons.

3. Weigh your pros and cons. Which ones are really important and which ones aren't critical?

4. Think about the tradeoffs you might need to make and add those to the mix.

TOPIC: _____

Pros	Cons

How was that for you? What did you discover? Did you have any *a-ha* moments?

You Don't Know What You Don't Know

Consider the following statement: *You don't know what you don't know.* In other words, are the areas that create discomfort stemming from areas in which you have no expertise or knowledge? If that last statement was confusing, let me back up a little with a short example.

I bought my first car after I graduated from college and found a job as an accountant. It was a lemon yellow 'vette. Don't get too excited—it was a Chevette, which even at the pinnacle of its existence was an ugly little box. But it was mine and I was thrilled to own a car. When it came time to service the car with a tune-up and oil change, I figured I could save some money and do it myself. Note to reader: My knowledge of auto mechanics was somewhere below zero. But I figured the guys in high school who worked in auto shop weren't rocket scientists, so ergo, I got this. I will spare you the gory and gruesome details. Suffice it to say that the cost of fixing what I screwed up far exceeded what it would have cost if I had let the dealer do it to begin with. Lesson learned: You don't know what you don't know until you're knee deep in wires and oil.

Getting back to the idea that we don't know what we don't know. This seems to be one of the biggest areas of concern and dissatisfaction. Let's examine this together because money is one area where lack of knowledge or comfort seems to hold a great deal of weight. There seems to be some confusion about where money knowledge comes from. Some families talk about money and teach important lessons about savings and prudent spending. Others, unfortunately, grow up in households where money is never discussed. Have you ever heard an elderly person share information about the health of someone, and if that person has cancer, the word is whispered at infrasonic levels? Well, for some, money is treated the same way. It might be because talking about money is considered rude or tacky, or that their messages about money is that it's no one's business, or that their own level of understanding is low and therefore there is embarrassment in broaching the subject. My statement to you is this: It is vital that you understand where your money beliefs come from, and how it impacts your behavior and habits. But when it comes to the technical sides of financial decisions, there is a whole different level of knowledge that is required.

Take life insurance, for example. Looking at something as "simple" as life insurance as an example of not knowing what you don't know, think about these questions:

- Do you need life insurance?
- How much coverage is appropriate?
- What risks are you most interested in covering?
- What type of insurance?
- For how long do you need protection?
- What company should you trust?
- By what criteria do you judge a company?
- How will you know if the company is going to fail?

- By what mode should you pay?
- Who should be the beneficiaries?
- If you have children, can they be the direct beneficiaries?
- Can you afford it?
- Can you afford not to have it?
- Should you buy it online or find an agent?
- Who can you trust to provide proper advice?
- What riders are important?
- If you're buying permanent protection, what dividend options are appropriate?
- What are the underwriting requirements?

Believe it or not, there are several more questions that need to be considered in just this one area. Is there any question why you might be experiencing a high degree of sleeplessness? Where there are unknowns, and you don't even know the scope of the unknowns, confusion and fear and maybe even shutdown are sure to follow.

Separating Technical Financial Knowledge From Beliefs and Behaviors

So your ability to comprehend the scope of all the financial issues that you need to deal with is less than comfortable. You need to be okay with the idea that if it is something you never learned, you should not expect to be comfortable. But that's all right: it makes you exactly *normal*. What we need to do is separate your beliefs and behaviors around money from your technical knowledge.

It is vitally important that you work toward a better understanding of you, your money history, your beliefs, behaviors, and habits around money. The technical stuff comes later.

I need you to make the decision to ignore the technical questions that keep you up at night and focus on the behavioral issues associated with your money life. All the technical knowledge in the world is not going to help your money life if you cannot control your spending and cannot change your habits to be more in alignment with your values.

|||||||||

The Pickle Jar Story

As far back as I can remember, the pickle jar sat on the floor beside the dresser in my parents' bedroom. When he got ready for bed, Dad would empty his pockets and toss his coins into the jar. As a small boy, I was always fascinated by the sounds the coins made as they were dropped into the jar. They landed with a merry jingle when the jar was almost empty. Then, the tones gradually muted to a dull thud as the jar was filled.

I used to squat on the floor in front of the jar and admire the copper and silver circles that glinted like a pirate's treasure when the sun poured through the bedroom window. When the jar was filled, Dad would sit at the kitchen table and roll the coins before taking them to the bank. Taking the coins to the bank was always a big production. Stacked neatly in a small cardboard box, the coins were placed between Dad and me on the seat of his old truck.

Each and every time as we drove to the bank, Dad would look at me hopefully. "Those coins are going to keep you out of the textile mill, son. You're going to do better than me. This old mill town's not going to hold you back." Also, each and every time, as he slid the box of rolled coins across the counter at the bank toward the cashier, he would grin proudly and say, "These are for my son's college fund. He'll never work at the mill all his life like me."

We would always celebrate each deposit by stopping for an ice cream cone. I always got chocolate. Dad always got vanilla. When the clerk at the ice cream parlor handed Dad his change, he would show me the few coins nestled in his palm. "When we get home, we'll start filling the jar again." He always let me drop the first coins into the empty jar. As they rattled around with a brief happy jingle, we grinned at each other. "You'll get to college on pennies, nickels, dimes, and quarters," he said. "But you'll get there. I'll see to that."

The years passed, and I finished college and took a job in another town. Once, while visiting my parents, I used the phone in their bedroom and noticed that the pickle jar was gone. It had served its purpose and had been removed.

A lump rose in my throat as I stared at the spot beside the dresser where the jar had always stood. My dad was a man of few words and never lectured me on the values of determination, perseverance, and faith.

The pickle jar had taught me all these virtues far more eloquently than the most flowery of words could have done. When I married, I told my wife, Susan, about the significant part the lowly pickle jar had played in my life as a boy. In my mind, it defined, more than anything else, how much my dad had loved me.

No matter how rough things got at home, Dad continued to doggedly drop his coins into the jar. Even the summer when Dad got laid off from the mill and Mama had to serve dried beans several times a week, not a single dime was taken from the jar. To the contrary, as Dad looked across the table at me, pouring catsup over my beans to make them more palatable, he became more determined than ever to make a way out for me. "When you finish college, Son," he told me, his eyes glistening, "you'll never have to eat beans again—unless you want to."

The first Christmas after our daughter Jessica was born, we spent the holiday with my parents. After dinner, Mom and Dad sat next to each other on the sofa, taking turns cuddling their first grandchild. Jessica began to whimper softly, and Susan took her from Dad's arms. "She probably needs to be changed," she said, carrying the baby into my parents' bedroom to change her diaper.

When Susan came back into the living room, there was a strange mist in her eyes. She handed Jessica back to Dad before taking my hand and leading me into the room. "Look," she said softly, her eyes directing me to a spot on the floor beside the dresser. To my amazement, there, as if it had never been removed, stood the old pickle jar, the bottom already covered with coins. I walked over to the pickle jar, dug down into my pocket, and pulled out a fistful of coins. With a gamut of emotions choking me, I dropped the coins into the jar. I looked up and saw that Dad, carrying Jessica, had slipped quietly into the room. Our eyes locked, and I knew he was feeling the same emotions I felt. Neither one of us could speak.

||||||||||

Ah, our values—our *real* values—not the ones that we tell ourselves are important, but those that reside deep within our hearts. "The Pickle Jar" is a great example of applying values to real action. In this case, the values created a set of beliefs, behaviors, and habits that supported that value. Technical knowledge and comfort did not play a part in building success. Many people value education, and therefore putting money away for their children to attend college sits very high on the list. They might get trapped in trying to analyze every possible 529 plan and do nothing, or they might start putting money into a savings account. You do not need a PhD in financial planning to create actions that bring you in alignment with your values. (In the next chapter we will explore your values or what I call, your *musts*.)

Rethinking Your Financial Discomforts: Getting to the *Whys*

Let's go back to the areas that create stress and those that create comfort. As you examine your pillow factor, uncover the areas that create stress or discomfort in your money life. We want to create a juxtaposed position in your thinking. For example: If you have difficulty controlling your spending, try to understand where this came from. What were the circumstances in your past that lead to difficulty in keeping the dollar in your pocket or the credit card in your wallet? If you think about this, you will most likely be able to draw a straight line between what you heard, saw, or experienced and how you act today.

People who grew up during the Depression generally fall into two categories: Either they will not part with a dime, or they are inveterate spenders. Their experiences create the pattern for their beliefs, behaviors, and habits. Some were so pained by their experience that fear took over making spending very painful; a "just in case" attitude took over. Others wound up bathing themselves in things to soothe the lack they once experienced.

I remember, vividly, my parents fighting bitterly about money. My father, a child of Depression, was hard-pressed to part with a nickel. My mother, 11 years his junior, was not a Depression child and had a completely different experience when it came to entitlements. It wasn't pretty. It took a long time for me to understand why I had a stomachache anytime the discussion of money was raised.

For some people, the idea of being able to spend freely is associated with how they feel about themselves and their self-esteem. For some, it might be that at one time in their life, they experienced lack and now they refuse to feel that pain of not being able to "have."

The idea here, and as demonstrated in "The Pickle Jar," is that it's about small change or small changes. But before you can approach the idea of change, you have to, as Simon Sinek put it, "start with why." You must define why you do anything; without this understanding, you are a rudderless ship untethered and uncontrolled by meaningful destination. It's a lousy way to live your life.

Let's connect the dots here.

- Our beliefs create our behaviors, and our behaviors create our habits around money.
- We may be either worriers or avoiders, which creates a pathway to either no decisions or less than optimal choices.
- Though we might have great discomfort around money and financial matters, there are simply too many issues to feel a sense of comfort—so we either do what is convenient or we do nothing. An example of that might

be signing up for employer-sponsored life insurance and believing that it is sufficient or failing to increase your 401(k) contributions as your salary increases.

- We generally do not take the time to really think about or talk about our values. But by making that effort, we create a set of "rules" that become our guideposts.

- ***With every decision you make, you are either moving closer to or further away from living your values.***

Let's try an exercise to start replacing negative behaviors with thoughts of more positive ones. Doing so can help you to think about how to make small, meaningful changes to improve your financial life and live your values.

In Worksheet 4-2 make a list of your current behaviors that keep your head off the pillow. For example:

1. I spend every penny I earn.
2. I don't think about how much I spend.
3. I have a high balance on my credit cards.
4. If I lose my job I cannot survive without outside help for more than a month or two.

Now, replace those behaviors with more positive messages. For example:

1. I would feel more at peace and comfortable if I was saving on a regular basis.
2. I carefully apportion my income to cover my needs and to provide for a secure future.

3. I live debt-free and have no pressure when the monthly bills come in.
4. I have a rational emergency fund saved that can see me through nine months of living while I transition into a new opportunity.

Time to get going on worksheets 4-2 and 4-3. Worksheet 4-2 will help you look at your current thoughts and likely replacements. Worksheet 4-3 is designed to help you organize your thoughts, and begin to align what is really important and what life is likely to look like if you don't.

Take all the time you need to get your thoughts together, and attack each question and topic as thoroughly as possible. You might find you will go back and add more thoughts, similar to your mind map from Chapter 3. That's great work!

WORKSHEET 4-2: REPLACING NEGATIVE BEHAVIORS WITH POSITIVE THOUGHTS

List your current negative behaviors:

1.

2.

3.

4.

Now think about how you can turn these negative behaviors into positives:

1.

2.

3.

4.

You need time, space, and focus to make this real and meaningful.

Once you've accumulated your list of replacement behaviors or guidelines, start to think about what small steps that you can take to move you in the right direction.

WORKSHEET 4-3: ORGANIZING YOUR THOUGHTS

Use your responses from Worksheet 4-2 to fill in the blanks here. The goals are to organize your thoughts and to begin to envision a new plan to move you forward.

- What do you need to stop doing?

- What do you need to start doing?

- Why is it mega-important that you do this?

- What is the cost of not changing?

- What will your life look like if you remain as is?

- What can your life look like if you make meaningful small shifts in your life that are aligned with your values?

CHAPTER 5

Your Soul Wants to Drive: Putting Your Values Into Motion

Considering our lives today, it's pretty evident that we have the attention span of a mosquito. Don't worry: It isn't really your fault. If you can focus long enough to follow my point, I think you'll get the drift. Add up the impact of technology, media, and the pressure to do more, make more, work more, see more, raise our children to Ivy League schools, and generally be perceived by our peers as the superhero of choice. It's no wonder then that our eyes and attention flit from smartphone to computer screen to whatever is in our way. Observe someone standing on line at the store or coffee shop or waiting for a bus—eyes glued to the screen, headphones on, trying to connect and, at the same time, remaining disconnected. There is no "there" there.

Multitasking is synonymous with how we conduct our lives. Unfortunately, the whole idea is completely impossible. Our brains are not wired to attend to more than one task at a time, unless you put walking and chewing gum at the same time as multitasking. One of the biggest challenges we face, from a societal basis, is our lack of time and focus to consider what we really care about most. We're too busy multitasking (or at least trying to) to be able to create a bridge between our life and our values. Trust me: They're in there somewhere. You just need a little time to unload all the stuff that is covering them up. It's like trying to find the matching sock in a pile of laundry. Rather than taking the time to fold everything from the top down, we wind up randomly grabbing bits and pieces, hoping to find the prize.

In this chapter, we will focus on your real values and how to separate out old beliefs that you've been dragging around from the stuff that makes your heart happy. Then we will look at your habits and examine whether they support your desire to live according to what you value most. You will zero in on your *musts*, and while you're on this journey, you will create the billboards of your life's values as a guide to keep you on track.

Slowing Down to Find Your *Musts* (and to Weed Out the *Shoulds*)

Charles and Diane knew that things had to change. While Charles made more-than-sufficient income, he was constantly working, trying to satisfy clients and colleagues alike. Charles's lack of attention to their overall financial health made Diane really uncomfortable. At a recent meeting, Diane was explaining her frustration, while Charles was busily engaged on his iPhone. The situation reached a boiling point as Diane hit her limit.

*"I can't take this anymore. We make appointments to come in and talk about **our** plan, but you can't give me more than 10 seconds of your time. This is nuts. We're wasting our time and money!"*

Charles looked up, not quite sure what was happening, only that there were several sets of eyes directing their attention his way.

"I have to make a living. Money doesn't just magically appear!" Charles said somewhat defensively.

As Diane was about to respond, I put my hand up to signal her to hold off. The meeting sank into silence. We know that the universe abhors a vacuum and it wasn't long before Charles put his iPhone away and turned to Diane.

"I'm sorry. You're right. It's so hard to focus when there are so many pressures to get things done."

It was my turn. "Okay, you two. Tell me: What must happen in your financial life to provide the comfort and satisfaction that is important to you?

Silence descended.

Diane started, "Wow. I haven't ever thought in terms of my musts. I need time to think about it."

Charles followed quickly with, "I must put my iPhone away if we're going to have this conversation."

Diane turned to Charles, her eyes showing signs of tears, "I need to know that if something happens to you, I won't be left in a mess. I need to know that, while I am raising our children, all your hard work means you will have a better life when you stop working. And I need to feel that we are working for the same goals."

|||||||||

You see, when it comes down to it, we all have our *musts*. When you get to the heart of the matter, it is first about security (remember our buddy Abe Maslow from Chapter 3?) and then attending to areas most valued.

"I don't want to outlive my resources." (That's a pretty good *must*, huh?)

"I don't want to be dependent on my children." (Pretty strong conviction.)

"I want to help pay for my grandchildren's college education." (Important dreams.)

"I want my children to be self-sufficient independent human-beings who help make the world better." (Legacy values.)

"I want my legacy to support the arts/my university/ medical research." (Soul-driven meaning.)

It is interesting to observe that in these examples of *musts*, there is no sense of 'keeping up with the Joneses or competition with anyone's brother-in-law. Your *musts* represent the statement of what must occur for you to feel secure, satisfied, and successful. The driver for these heart-centered needs is an individual's values. We value, for example, security, our family, our causes, and the aspects of life for which we are ***willing*** to make changes.

In order for us to set our journey on the right course, we first need to know where we are going and why we are going there. Think about taking a trip from the United States to Thailand. What do you need to consider before you embark? Why are you going? Even if it's to eat lobster on the beach for $1, you need a reason to go through the process of travel. Do you have a passport? Do you need a visa? What are the costs? How long a trip will your life and resources allow? Do you need any inoculations? What are the costs of flights? Where will you stay? Do you need to find a tour guide? You get the point. Unfortunately, too many people spend more energy arranging their vacation than they spend on considering their values and making sure they are taking the right steps.

Time for an exercise. Worksheet 5-1 asks you to think about your values/your *musts*. You might have one or more. Take some time to think about what's supremely important to you. Remember: These values are *yours*, not mine, not those of your parents, siblings, or spouse—just yours alone.

A note to consider before you begin: We live in a world of *shoulds* and self-imposed or societally-imposed guilt. If there's a *should* in your thinking, it's not your *must*. For example: I *should* provide an inheritance to my nephew because my sister would be mad if I didn't. This is a guilt-based want (or *should*), not a values-based *must*.

WORKSHEET 5-1: IDENTIFYING YOUR *MUSTS*

Write down your true values, your absolute *musts.* You should not have more than three, because it's vital that you hone in on just those super, top-of-the-list, right-to-your-heart values. (Hint: A Rolex or designer handbag should not be one of them.)

1.

2.

3.

Great. How do those look? Are you *sure* they are your *musts?*

If so, what are you willing to do to ensure they happen? Would you spend less today? Save more? Contribute to a retirement plan? Work an extra job? Change your lifestyle?

If you are willing to make changes in your lifestyle today to ensure success, then you are dead on: They are your *musts.*

If you are unwilling to make changes, then you might have missed the mark. Before you continue, take more time to think about what is most important to you. In case you are concerned, you are allowed to change your answers. After all, this is your exploration; I am merely the guide.

Are You Moving in the Right Direction?

Now that you have your *musts*, those enunciations of **your values**, you have a little more work to do.

A few words about habits. Aristotle said, "We are what we repeatedly do." And who is prepared to argue with him? Habits become a part of us, our normal go-to behavior, like holding your toothbrush in your dominant hand or putting on socks before pants. They aren't important, thought out, or planned; they just have become our default. Changing habits can feel like climbing Mt. Everest naked in the dead of winter. So, why do it alone? No, I am not referring to climbing Mt. Everest naked in the dead of winter. I am referring to changing habits. It's good to have someone along to walk the journey with you. Having a strong support system is key to success. If you have been a advocate of retail therapy that has added to your problems, you probably are not going to get much support from someone else who is a shopaholic, especially as you are building new supportive success habits. It's just too tempting, and who needs that constant reminder of what you're "missing"? In fact, you're embarking on building your happiness and living rationally. Who are the people with whom you share values? They are the people you want to model and lean on. Maybe it means you need to expand your scope of friends to include those who are less acquisition-focused. There is a need for fearlessness in moving outside of how others have seen you. By surrounding yourself with those whose values are aligned with yours, you create mutual support and strengthen your resolve.

You might want to consider taking the time you previously spent in acquisition mode (aka shopping) and volunteer that time to those less fortunate or in dire need of your help (a library, a hospital, the elderly, and so forth). Gratitude is a great way to focus on what really matters. Remember: Positive habits bring you closer to you living your *musts*.

The next part of your assignment is to use Worksheet 5-2 to review the areas of your life that are compatible or incompatible with your *musts*.

WORKSHEET 5-2: DO YOUR HABITS SUPPORT YOUR VALUES?

Think about and write down those habits that support your ability to live your values. In other words, what works well and what can you celebrate in your money life? *Examples: "I do not spend more than I can comfortably pay off each month." "I save/invest X% of my paycheck every time I get paid before I spend a penny."*

1.

2.

3.

Now think about and write down those habits that detract from your ability to live your values. For example, do you spend frivolously? Do you refrain from saving because it will impact the discretionary part of your life?

1.

2.

3.

Think about the costs of not altering your habits. What doesn't happen? Will your *musts* be attainable if you remain doing what you do today?

1.

2.

3.

What or who supports habits that negatively impact your success? For example, do you have a friend or relative who wants a "partner in crime"? Or do you believe that making changes will impact your relationships negatively?

1.

2.

3.

Setting a New Course: Forming Habits That Support Your Money *Musts*

So you see, we devote so much time and energy on the day-to-day stuff, we don't have the time, energy, or focus to think about what we *really* desire most. There is a commitment necessary to create a shift in your habits. This brings us back to the conversation in Chapter 3 about our beliefs and behaviors. Our shifted habits become an extension of what we believe and thus the tools to transport us from money misery to a feeling of empowerment and real richness.

Habits are the active part of our belief system. We acquire habits as soon as we can understand: Brush your teeth before bed, wash your hands, say thank you. These actions become ingrained in us. We believe them, consciously or subconsciously, and act out what we believe. Think about a time when your habits supported you. Maybe you are in tip-top physical shape and exercise five to six times a week; you attend to strength training, cardio training, and body flexibility. Your habits of going to the gym, hitting the Stairmaster, and getting down on the mat at a yoga class are all habits that support good health.

You can use ideal supportive habits to help you consider what unsupportive habits need adjustment. Think about what happened to shift you from eating fast food to making more healthy food choices. You made a decision and acted because you valued the benefits of a healthy body more than the greasy "goodness" of junk food. It might have taken you months until you could pass a Wendy's without salivating, but you don't even think about it now. In fact, you might not even remember the last time, it's become so natural for you to eat healthily.

We need to build strong habits that support our aims, whether it's to lose weight, get in shape, get to work on time, or study to master new information or to build financial security.

Creating Your Personal Money Billboards to Keep You on Track

Now that you have done the great work of articulating your *musts*, complete Worksheet 5-3 to come up with some powerful headlines that can help reinforce your mission. Your money billboards are statements that make your *musts* real and meaningful. For example:

"Money is a tool for achieving financial security."

"I know the difference between my wants and my needs."

"I will live more abundantly without the weight of credit card debt on my head."

"Living within my means enables me to save for the future and appreciate the security that provides."

Get the point? Write some headlines that you can read, reread, and re-reread. These empowering statements are super-important to remind you to be mindful of your task. Without the support, you might become the dieter who eats nothing but celery sticks for two weeks before diving headfirst into a gallon of Ben and Jerry's.

WORKSHEET 5-3: YOUR MONEY BILLBOARDS

Come up with three headlines to help reinforce your values and keep you on the path to success.

1.

2.

3.

Read your headlines throughout the day: when you get up, mid-morning, at lunchtime, mid-afternoon, at dinnertime, before bed. The more frequently you remind yourself, the stronger you become. Put a reminder on your calendar or phone to take out your headlines and read them. Each time, add another drop of energy and strength toward attaining your preferred future.

|||||||||

You've done great work, focusing on what must happen in your life and separating out the needs from the wants. These foundational blocks allow you to create awesome supportive habits.

CHAPTER 6

Adjusting Your Money Mindset

Mindset is defined by the *Oxford Dictionary* as: "The established set of attitudes held by someone." A money mindset is then the established set of attitudes about money held by someone. We all have our own money mindset. If your money mindset works for you by establishing a set of positive beliefs, it becomes self-empowering. If your money mindset is rife with negative messages, it can lead to a lifetime of being a slave to one's money history. Altering your money mindset to be positive and constructive will feel like a fresh breeze on a warm night; you feel alive and possess something wonderful, empowering, and precious. You've discovered that whatever you once believed doesn't have to belong to you, and you can add it to the list of lessons learned the hard way. You have discovered control over self, instead of existing on autopilot.

As you re-create your life, think of yourself as the sculptor, armed with a chisel to chip away all the unnecessary material to reveal a life that is not only affirming but self-loving. You can become the evangelist for money sanity and share your newly found understanding with those you love.

In this chapter, you will see examples of money mindsets and their impact. You will also explore long-term versus short-term mindsets and the all-important "how to begin" to shift your mindset to create more satisfying results, and look at a few examples of living richly. You will also have the opportunity to continue to create the foundation of what makes you feel rich. Take a few good breaths and be prepared to vanquish the internal foes that are standing between you and your ability to live your gloriously meaningful values.

Examples of Money Mindsets That Need a Second Look

Without the slightest conscious idea, we carry with us beliefs, born out of experience, that bend our thinking into alignment with what we come to know as "normal." We don't think about our money mindset; it's just there. Here are a couple examples of money mindsets that created money misery and conflict and the adjustments that had to be made.

|||||||||||

Casey, a 32-year-old single woman, sought help to work out some cash flow issues. It soon became apparent that there was more to it than helping her create a system.

"I am paying off my law school loans and I never seem to have enough money to live. I work a lot of long hours and I could use your help in guiding me to make some adjustments."

"Great. Tell me a little about you, your situation, and whatever else you believe would be helpful for me to understand."

"I get paid a salary and bonus. The salary is good, but the bonus is what helps me catch up and pay off my cards. The bonus is once a year, paid in January, but from the looks of things, I don't know how I can make it until then. Between the school loans, monthly bills and credit cards, I feel really squeezed. Plus, I never know what the bonus is going to be and that just adds to the pressure."

"Let's talk about options. Do you have savings? Do you get any support from your family?"

The word family *set off an unexpected maelstrom.*

"Support from my family? I wouldn't even know how to ask them. Money was always a super-secret thing. It was never spoken about. I mean, we lived okay, but, I don't think I can go to them about this. And no, I have no savings, just kind of going hand to mouth until bonus when I pay everything off and get straight with the world. My biggest worry is if the bonus is less than last year!"

"Casey, help me understand. What would be the ideal outcome for you here, other than us waving a magic wand

and making all the bills disappear? What do you value most? What must happen for you to feel secure?"

"Value most? Well, after I get my January bonus, I would have answered, 'A trip to St. Bart's,' but here we are in July and my answer is, peace of mind that I am not destroying myself. I work too hard to not have security. That must happen!"

|||||||||

Casey's story was also pretty typical. Parents who don't talk about money, shroud the issue in mystery. Instead of fostering healthy communication about savings, security, and wise spending, they leave children to their own devices and many times, there is a lack of valuation or real focus, because the topics have always remained obscure.

After a crash course in money basics and budgeting, Casey was able to see that the idea of just floating along this way was a river to misery and disaster. Casey created her cash flow, and together we devised a plan that included moving to a less-expensive apartment, canceling a planned vacation, and restructuring her debt. Casey decided that in order to live to her values and build security, she was going to put a moratorium on spending for all nonessential items and set a target to build an emergency fund to cover nine months of living expenses and then enroll in the firm 401(k) plan.

|||||||||

Pam and Henry, in their mid-50s, after putting their two children through college, were in desperate straits. They both earned decent incomes. Retirement was on their minds but the gap between their current savings and their cash flow needs was pretty vast. In reviewing their spending, it became obvious that their discretionary spending was out of control. Henry liked to play golf and Pam hadn't met a sale she didn't like. Henry, with a look of bitterness, said, "You have filled up every closet in the house with clothes, and yet it seems there is no end to the purchases." Pam's retort was just as bitter: "You can spend all that money on golf. You buy all the newest equipment and the carts, and greens fees are a fortune. So don't tell me about overspending."

"Let's take a step back, you guys." I said. "You're either in this together, or you're not. Tell me, Pam, What worries you the most about your financial life?"

Pam paused. "What will happen if either of us loses our job? We're sunk. How can we ever think of retiring? We can't save beyond our modest contributions to our retirement plans. I feel like we'll have to work forever and never enjoy our children or grandchildren. I cannot be a burden to my children. Oh, this is terrible!" With that the tears began.

The next part of the conversation centered on their money history. Henry grew up in a fairly affluent family that broke apart in divorce and dysfunction. He believed that spending money on his pleasures was something that was just the way it was supposed to be. Pam's family was different in that they struggled more financially, and her mother was very big on taking advantage of sales. So whenever the sign went up, purchases were made. Pam was aware that other families had more, but money was never talked about. Her earliest memories were about shopping and her mother's "nervousness" to buy when items went on sale. It all made sense.

"It seems like you've assimilated beliefs growing up that you've maintained without challenge. Do you believe they still work for you?" I asked.

Henry snorted, "Obviously not. But what can we do about it? It's who we are."

Meeting Henry's eyes, I replied, "It's who you both have been. Whether you continue that way is a choice."

||||||||||

Long-Term vs. Short-Term Money Mindset

Our money mindset is reflected by our actions; it's not something we even think about. To save or to spend, to think about today or tomorrow, hits our brain synapses in a flash. We know what we want. Have you ever stood at a checkout line at a grocery store and spied your favorite candy bar? A positive health mindset ignores the candy bar in favor of a more nutritious alternative. A mindset that heeds the subconscious instinct will wind up eating the candy bar while you're walking out of the store. Do you see the analogy? A well-conceived money mindset is aligned with your real values, but one that operates without consideration and purpose will constantly make decisions that work against your true values.

Think of it like a chess player. You look for the long-term result. That is your mindset, and you are willing to sacrifice a pawn or two to capture your opponent's king. A strong, present, and aware mindset is like that of the successful chess player, willing to sacrifice a Milky Way bar for long-term health or maybe for that piece of amazing, fine Jacques Torres chocolate you received as a gift, waiting at home. Hmmmm. . . What to do? What to do?

Does the term *delayed gratification* make you queasy? You might ascribe to the school of thought that says, "I may die tomorrow, so why put off for tomorrow what I might enjoy today?" One of my favorites, "I live in the moment," is the supreme cop-out and actually abuses the meaning and intention. To *live in the moment* is to be aware of yourself, everything from your breath, to your feet on the floor, to the lightning-quick thoughts racing through your brain. To *be* in the moment means to experience the moment. Transcendental Meditation talks about the idea of awareness of your thoughts and the nonattachment to those thoughts. Being aware is different from acting on whims and falling prey to modern marketing techniques.

Making Adjustments to Your Money Mindset

I was stunned upon seeing advertising on Facebook for items I had been looking at on another site. "Well, look here. How the heck did they know I was just looking at those running shoes?" Not only are we in a battle with our internal broken mindsets, but external foes are hooked into every Website or search engine inquiry we make, tracking our tastes, wants, and desires.

It is not a helpless battle. In fact, it's highly winnable if you monitor and adjust your mindset, and apply techniques intentionally structured to help you get through the inevitable tests. Remember: The goal is to match your values with your beliefs and behaviors that become your new and improved mindset. There is no switch to turn or card to activate, it's your decision, your actions, and your life.

Look around. You know where you are; you're *here*. After all the work we've done thus far, I think you have a pretty good idea of where *there* is. *There* is not a place, but a mindset matched appropriately with positive actions. *Here* is where you go from—not to. The journey of examining your current money mindset, your habits, and your awareness, and replacing what is working against your self-defined *musts*, is not a straight line—not one size fits all, not throw the switch on autopilot. It is a weaving, twisting, bumpy, and sometimes-harrowing experience of self-discovery and growth toward a more gratifying life.

If you have lived any reasonable amount of time believing and acting under a specific set of thoughts that have caused dissatisfaction and pain, well, it's time to consider the pain of change versus the pain of remaining as you are. Building satisfaction comes from awareness of your growing competence. Think of a toddler pulling herself up on shaky legs, only to go crashing down. While caught up in the sheer adorableness of the situation, you might have missed the fact that failure happens, until such time as competency is achieved. The baby stands, falls, stands, falls, stands, takes a step, falls, stands, takes a step or two, falls—you get the picture. Each time the child falls, words of encouragement and support assist her in getting back up and trying again, regardless of the six previous attempts that resulted in face plants. Within a short time this miniature person is flying around the house on two pretty self-assured legs. It's no different with anything new you seek to master.

Like learning an instrument or any other skill, it takes work, practice, failure, and the decision to keep going because the final goal is that glorious sound that comes out when success is achieved.

To get there you need the following:

1. A rational set of goals. The goals can be big and audacious, but rational, too.
2. The reason why this *must* happen. Without your reason—your values—it won't work.
3. Knowledge commensurate with the challenge. You need a commitment to learning that which you don't currently know.
4. The willingness to fail temporarily. Everyone fails, but resilient people get up and try again.
5. An overriding belief in your success. If you don't really believe it, why do it? Besides, your chance of success is less than remote.
6. Love and respect for yourself. If you can't love yourself, there are bigger problems than money.
7. A sense of humor. It helps when missteps occur. We take ourselves way too seriously.

A little humor can go a long way to shake off the "I'm a failure" inner rant.

8. Determination: getting past the negative self-talk, the external pressure, and the temptation. It's hard enough making changes, but beating yourself up en route is just unnecessary self-destruction.

Change is evolutionary by nature and practice. It's rarely easy, but what is worthwhile, important, and necessary is worth the effort. Tripping on a step is easy (trust me: I know this), making life-altering amendments to your thoughts, beliefs, and actions is a tad more challenging.

Once you decide, and I mean *really* decide, that the track you are running on is heading for the cliff and that without a change in course, the outcome will not be pretty, you can begin to build, bit-by-bit, the components necessary to effect real change.

Begin with *belief*. Make it a strong statement. For example: "I will live debt-free and create security for myself and my family."

Test that belief against your current reality. "Right now, I am burdened with debt, but by careful consistent and meaningful actions, I can eliminate the debt and begin to build financial security."

Create small steps that lean in a more positive direction, including the necessary support. "I will pay down my debt every week by taking 5 percent of my income and putting it toward my debt. Further, I will cut my discretionary spending and use those savings towards debt elimination."

Spending decisions are constant, and buying opportunities are ceaseless. What steps can you take to limit the decisions or eliminate the pressure? Dissect the specific steps necessary and set your plan in motion.

Monitor your progress constantly. Keep a log of your challenges, your decisions, and your outcomes. Celebrate what went right; if the outcome wasn't ideal, ask yourself what steps might have brought about a different (better) result. Self-punishment, blame, shame, and negativity are pointless and counterproductive. Haven't you been beating yourself up enough all these years?

Change is about starting and stopping. In order to support growth and move closer to your values, you need to determine what you need to **start** doing different, with the firm understanding of why and that same firm understanding of what you need to **stop** doing. Both those actions bring you closer to your goals, your security and your dreams of a life aligned with your highest values. Remember your money billboards.

Deserving Richness: Examples of Living Richly

There's a difference between being rich and living richly, just as the definition of wealth differs depending on the point of view. There are those who live simply, without many possessions to demonstrate their power, prestige, and wealth. The values they possess are far more important than the car they drive, and whether or not they own a private jet or yacht, but rather what they do in and for their family and the world.

Ted and Jackie were considering retirement when we met. Ted worked for a well-known tech firm and earned a very substantial income, including stock options and generous bonuses. Ted and Jackie lived simply in a nice home in a nice neighborhood. Both of their daughters worked part-time jobs during high school and over the summers to provide money for books and sundry spending during college. After reviewing their financial position, I asked what they want their retirement to look like. What was important to them, to make their lives worthwhile, important, and meaningful?

They looked at each other, and Jackie spoke. "We want to become docents in the National Park System and give tours, live in cabins and tents, and be in nature."

Ted spoke next, noticing my look of surprise. "Yes, I know we can afford to buy vacation homes and travel around the world, but honestly, we just want a simple life. We have put away enough for our daughters' college and some left over to pay for a wedding. Our financial responsibilities are taken care of. We just want to live, breathe clean air, and enjoy our time together."

Values.

Sam and Trish are a multigenerational couple with a young child. Sam, having been divorced for many years, met Trish, and though their ages were pretty dissimilar, their values were not. Sam, who worked hard and lived frugally, was thinking about retirement. When I asked Sam about retirement he told me of his years in the Peace Corps, working with families without adequate shelter, without clean water, and with no medical facilities at their disposal.

Sam said, "I have a roof over my head, my family, and clean water. I don't need or want more stuff in my life. I love spending time with Trish and our son. Retirement will afford me that opportunity and my lack of financial burdens has allowed me to live without worry."

Values.

Anna, a widow, raised three boys and, as she puts it, a husband. She has eight grandchildren and gets great joy from family get-togethers. She never misses a soccer or base-ball game, except when there are conflicting game times, and has a wonderful relationship with her sons and her daughters-in-law. She's not wealthy, but she describes herself as the richest woman in the world. She volunteers three days a week at various organizations that fills her with accomplishment and joy.

Values.

Steve, age 34, has paid off his school loans and has no debt. He works hard and even has a second part-time job that allows him to save a little more. He lives modestly and is preparing for his upcoming wedding. Steve and Emily both love to go camping and, rather than spend big bucks on a trip to Hawaii, they're heading for the hills, with backpacks and tents, to hike parts of the Appalachian Trail. They planned an outdoor wedding in the woods and invited their family and friends to attend wearing appropriate attire. (Bug spray will be provided.)

Values.

What do *you* care most about?

Beginning the Work to Live Your Own Rich Life

Benjamin Franklin, at age 20, created a system to work on his character and what he valued in being the best person he could be. His list of 13 values included temperance, silence, order, resolution, frugality, sincerity, moderation, humility, and tranquility. Franklin would select those traits and actively work on them for periods of time, exercising his will and training his ability to live to his credo and goals. Benjamin Franklin believed in *actively* working on improving himself by focusing on what he valued.

Let's exercise our internal Bens by thinking about and developing your values: In Worksheet 6-1, you're going to explore your thoughts about a rich life. You will want to review your values worksheets from Chapter 3 and Chapter 5. In addition, you want to review the work on **needs** versus **wants**.

WORKSHEET 6-1: WHAT MAKES YOU FEEL RICH?

Define the riches in your life. In other words, what and who do you value above everything?

- Do you feel rich when you have the clarity to make decisions (Yes/No)? Why?

- Do you feel rich when you have options and choices (Yes/No)? Why?

- Do you feel rich when money is not a top-of-mind worry when something unexpected happens (Yes/No)?

- Is someone else's (apparent) wealth a factor in whether you feel rich (Yes/No)? Why?

- How do you deal with the feelings of needing immediate gratification and reward: (Yes/No)

Do you cave?

Do you compromise?

Do you fight off the "hunger"?

Do you need a reward for resisting the urge?

Fill in the following with short answers:

I feel in control when   .

I value more than anything else: .

I am at my best when   .

I have experienced success in my life when   .

I felt rich when   .

Write an example for each of the above short answers you completed. Tell the story behind your answer. For example, when you were at your best, what were the circumstances, how did it happen, how did you feel, why, etc.? Be as explicit and complete as possible. Write the story of your richness and successes.

Can you see that your money mindset is the bedrock or underpinning of your success? You have experienced success in various ways during your life. It doesn't matter if you are a CEO or work on a farm, you have tasted and experienced success in some form along the way.

Consider what you have learned over your lifetime. Apply the success stories to a successful money mindset. Think **needs** first: What do you *need* in order to have the safety, security, and basic attributes that will lead you, step-by-step, to your rich life?

Can you see how distractions created by "things," experiences, lack of knowledge, money history, insecurity, and judgments can impact your money mindset and cloud your vision?

Can you see a path to a positive money mindset?

||||||||||

In the next chapter we begin to create a support structure, review your numbers, and begin to make your money plan. The idea is to apply your well-crafted values to the numbers and start moving forward. Onward—strongly!

CHAPTER 7

Chart Your Plan

Change is hard. There is no doubt that tearing down old beliefs and habits and rebuilding from the foundation up is a mighty challenge. What makes it even more potentially difficult is that, not only are we going down to the foundation, we are smashing through parts of the foundation that are cracked or crumbling or downright broken. But hey, what else have you got to do on a Tuesday?

You might be asking yourself, about now, why the heck you are doing this deep dive into your money history and your current behaviors. The answer might be sleeping in the next room, or it might be staring you right in the face when you stand in front of the mirror. And, are you ready for this? Consider that future generations will also be positively impacted by the great strides you make in reshaping your beliefs, behaviors, habits, and mindset.

You doubt my statement? Think of how you learned about money, the lessons learned in childhood, and how that shaped your life today. The same held true for your parents and their parents and on and on. We pass on our beliefs to our children, regardless of whether they are positive or not. Do you wish to relegate your children to the same broken beliefs and experiences, or provide them with a healthier, more balanced, and satisfying model for living without the negative influences? **By creating a new set of beliefs, you then have the opportunity to create a new future for yourself, your children, and for future generations.** It's a veritable avalanche of good stuff!

Regardless of whether you are the consummate avoider or the constant worrier, or your past beliefs or actions have led you to crisis, you can and must confront and deal with these beliefs and sink them into the circular file like Michael Jordan draining a three. Who we are today doesn't have to relegate us to a lifetime sentence of misery. We can become the creative force to be something better for ourselves, our loved ones, and future generations.

In this chapter, you will begin to chart the plan for your new financial future. The first stop is your "moment of truth," kind of like which fork in the road you will take. Next, you will begin to focus on creating your life by design, and the foundational statements on which your new life is built. You will again go back to the numbers because, without financial truth, it's all just words. Lastly, you will learn to activate the words, numbers, values, and goals to create a pathway for doing.

The Moment of Truth

Life by design is a concept of awareness, acceptance, and the willingness to replace old, broken ideas with more positive ones—you know, like the new billboards you wrote in Chapter 5 and are reading multiple times a day. (You *are* reading them, right?) This story is a great example of coming to a moment of truth, where a lifetime of guilt and destructive messages come face to face with the possibilities of change.

||||||||||

Ted and Giselle, a couple in their late 50s, are in a financial mess. Their work situation is unstable and they have amassed a massive pile of consumer debt. To put it bluntly, their situation is dire: too much debt, not enough income.

Giselle sits in front of a stack of papers enumerating each and every aspect of their financial woes. She is looking at the numbers. Ted is looking at nothing. The only way I can describe his expression is defeated.

I start the meeting the way I do each new encounter: asking, "How can I help?" What I hear from Ted is a long and self-blaming tale of disaster about how he single-handedly failed his wife and grown children. He places all the responsibility for their hardship on his own head. If there was a club nearby, he would have bludgeoned himself senseless.

After a solid 10 minutes of listening, I interrupt his self-flagellation and ask him to pass me a plastic-wrapped biscotti from the canister on the conference room table. My request baffles him, and he hesitantly complies. I take the biscotti, lean forward and use the biscotti to tap him on each shoulder. Looking him in the eyes I say, "I absolve you of all your sins."

Confused, he glances over to his wife and then at me. "Now that you have been absolved, are you ready to change your view from dwelling on the past to thinking about the future and possible solutions?"

The meeting dealt with hard truths. Ted was so immersed in his own suffering and the suffering he had put his family through that there was literally no space for him to create a new, more positive reality.

Me: "So, Ted, you have devoted the last 10 minutes of the meeting telling me how terrible you are and all the problems you caused by your habits. I get it. Mistakes have been made. But we are here now *and I believe it would be more useful to talk about where we are going rather than where we've been. Agreed?"*

Ted: "Yes, the weight of the past is debilitating. It would be great to focus on something else. But, honestly, I don't know where to begin."

Me: "Super, you don't have to know. I do; that's my job. Your job is for you and Giselle to think about: How would your life be different if you were debt-free?"

(long pause)

Giselle: "Wow, imagining having no debt, no calls, no pressure from bill collectors would be like heaven."

Ted: "I think I could look at my family and not feel like a failure."

Me: "Great. Sit with that for a minute, let it sink in, and marinate in your hearts and minds. Imagine you are debt-free, you are not getting harassing phone calls, and you are in control of your money life."

(another four- or five-minute pause)

Ted and Giselle sat there, eyes closed, tears began to flow.

Giselle: "Do you think it's possible?"

Ted: "It has to be, right? I mean, we cannot go on this way. We have to make this happen."

Giselle: "There is no other option."

Ted nodded.

||||||||||

It was a moment of truth, in which no other possibility existed; despite the pain, the change, the denial, the shifts, there was no turning back.

In order to arrive at your moment of truth, you must create such powerful reasons for change that there simply isn't any better option, even taking into account the pain that will be involved in making changes. Imagine your life without change, without focusing on your true values. What does that look like?

Don't like pain? Who does? But know that by remaining the same, the pain, while perhaps deferred a bit, will inevitably be *disastrous!* You can't hope or wish it away; your life-long broken money mindset is like a slow-growing cancer that will eventually destroy your ability to live your values. Worksheet 7-1 provides you with an opportunity to create some powerful ideas on your money mindset and your values.

WORKSHEET 7-1: HABITS, STAKEHOLDERS, AND YOUR PLAN

It's time to think, ponder, conceive, and create several statements that are facts:

1. Create a list that contains the ideas of your newly designed life. For example:

    - I am the happiest when I feel financially secure.
    - I feel great when my habits bring me closer to leading the life I deserve.
    - My family and I work together to save wisely, spend rationally, and give generously.
    - I value peace of mind above "things."
    - It's vital that I pass on healthy money beliefs and habits to those I love by setting an example that aligns my values with my actions.

2. Strengthen your defenses. Unless you have immense
    willpower, you need help.

    Who are the stakeholders who are most vested
    in these life-changing shifts? Who needs to be
    considered in building your success (for example,
    your spouse, partner, parent, child, friend)? Write
    their names and why they are stakeholders.

3. Chart your progress.

    Put it in writing. Make a graph. Create a chart.
    Keep a diary. Do whatever it takes to see how you
    are moving in the right direction.

    Here's an example: If you are paying down debt,
    make a payment every time you get paid. Keep a
    spreadsheet or list showing each payment and the
    shrinking balance.

    If you are trying to accumulate, the same strategy
    applies. Record every addition, no matter how small.

Let's say you have coupons to use for your groceries, and you save $14; that amount should be sent to your goal. The same applies for things like savings when gasoline prices come down, savings from elimination of non-valued expenses (i.e., you eliminate cable TV packages in favor of a less-expensive option). Each small change creates an opportunity to save more or retire debt more quickly. There's no shame in not having every cable channel or in using coupons or promotional opportunities.

4. Have accountability: Without accountability, we are prone to fall back to old habits. That's why there are coaches, trainers, counselors, therapists, and advisors galore.

    To whom will you be accountable? With what frequency? (I recommend every week to start for the first six months.)

Sometimes, we resist asking for help, usually because of fear and pride. If you wrestle with the idea of asking for help, especially in the area of personal finance, it is yet another obstacle in your path to living richly in alignment with your true values. At this point, you should be thinking, "Well, if you put it *that* way, I guess I can reach out and get help where I need it."

Think about what areas require the most help. If it's technical (for example, understanding why to take out a 15-year mortgage versus a 30-year, or what your asset allocation should be in your 401(k) plan), there are plenty of resources online, such as the National Endowment of Financial Education (www.NEFE.org), your local Financial Planning Association (www.FPAnet .org), and the National Association of Personal Financial Advisors (www.NAPFA.org). There are books galore, such as *Financial Fitness Forever* by Paul Merriman and Richard Buck, and local adult education courses. Avoid any book that touts "Easy Steps." There's nothing blatantly easy and by presenting it as such demeans those who have very limited financial knowledge. Like learning anything, it takes time and desire.

Note of warning: Avoid the seminars sponsored by Insurance salesmen and stockbrokers (even if they have CFP certifications). These seminars, aka rubber chicken dinners where you go for a free meal, are a cheesy attempt to get unsuspected folks in a room to sell them annuities, life insurance, or other investment schemes.

If the help you need is more in line with psychological counseling, there's the American Psychological Association (www.APA.org) or National Alliance of Professional Psychology Provisers (www.NAPPP.org). Talk to your physician about a referral to a highly regarded therapist. As I said in the beginning of the book, I am not a therapist, but it seems to me that those who practice cognitive behavior therapy (CBT) might be most aligned to building new and strong habits.

Taking Small Steps to Get Into SHAPE

Each step forward, closer to security, is movement in the direction most important to you, your family, and your values. We call it getting into SHAPE: Savor—Honor—Appreciate—Praise—Exalt all your great work. Maybe this seems silly to you, but the research is clear. People who have positive reinforcement and support are more likely to be successful than those who don't. So bathe in the Praise, marinate in Appreciation, and soak in the Savoring. It's necessary and important to feel that each small step has meaning.

Avoid at all costs the "it's only . . ." thinking or rationalizing. That attitude minimizes your efforts and renders the dollars as irrelevant, rather than vitally important. Remember: We're rebuilding habits. The $5 savings may not be the difference between success and failure, but it is a step *toward* your goal, not a step *away.*

Begin each discussion, whether internal or verbal, with the following: "Does this action bring me closer to or further away from my goal?"

If the answer is, "Well, it's only . . ." or "It doesn't matter," ask yourself whether that is true. It may be; but then again, it might not be. Remember: Just because you think something is true, doesn't make it so. Think of someone being on an eating plan designed to reduce their weight. If eating one cookie is irrelevant to the goal, so be it, as long as it doesn't devolve into eating a box of cookies that wind up adding weight rather than reducing.

It's not the one-time treat that will defeat you, it's the belief that change will happen without having to deal with internal resistance and external forces (you know, the person that waves the jelly doughnut under your nose when you're being good). You can bend (in fact, that's good), but understand the difference between bending and breaking—like where you do a gainer in pike position into the dish of brownies.

Your Money Facts

Way back in Chapter 1, you gathered your financial information. Well, it's time to go back to that worksheet. What you want to do now is reconnect with the numbers. Thus far, you have been walking in a more ethereal landscape; now it's time to return your attention, perhaps with a more aware mindset, to the numbers that impact your financial life. Remember: As you learn and more ideas begin to crystalize, go back to your mind map and keep fleshing it out. The more detailed the better.

Beginning with, as Stephen Covey says, the end in mind, you know what your ultimate objective looks like. Right? A life by design, structured to align with your desire for security and choices, and centered on the values you hold dearest is the goal. When it comes to your money, there are two main areas to consider: how much you make and how much you spend. Worksheet 7-2 will take another look at your income and whether you have the ability to increase the top line. Then, you will re-examine your expenses and separate out what is fixed, marginally controllable, and completely discretionary so that you spot areas where change is possible. Time to crawl inside the numbers, this time with greater awareness.

WORKSHEET 7-2: SPOTTING OPPORTUNITIES FOR IMPROVEMENTS IN YOUR FINANCES

Answer the following questions and fill in the blanks to get a clear picture of your income and where it's going. *Tip:* Use the numbers from worksheets 1-2 and 1-3 where you can to save yourself some time.

1. How much do you earn?

2. What are your sources of income?

3. Can you earn more?

4. Are you able to supplement your main income with additional earning?

Note: When I talk about income supplementing, I am not talking about "get rich quick" Internet schemes, work at home on Twitter, or other such scams meant to separate you further from your hard-earned scratch. I am talking about a part-time job that will add to the "In" column.

Now let's go over to that outflow side of the ledger. Remember the work you did way back in Chapter 1 to get a handle on your numbers?

Rather than just listing expenses, think in terms of five different categories:

1. Fixed costs: rent/mortgage payment, real estate taxes, condo maintenance, etc.

2. Marginally controllable costs: groceries, utilities, prescriptions, insurance premiums. (These are expenses that can be controlled to a degree based on your ability to make better decisions.)

3. Completely discretionary: vacations, entertainment etc.

4. Debt service: credit cards, school loans, etc.

5. Taxes: federal, state, and local taxes withheld from your salary; estimated taxes paid or balance due from the previous year. (If you received a refund, deduct it from the total of taxes paid.)

Cash Flow		
Year		
	Monthly	**Annually**
Inflow:		
Sources of Income:		
Primary Employment—Gross	$	$
Secondary Employment		
Gifts		
Other (bonus, etc.)		
Total Inflows (A)	$	$
Outflows:		
Fixed Expenses:		
Mortgage/RE Taxes/Rent	$	$
Maintenance Fees		
Other		
Other		
Total Fixed Expenses (B)	$	$
Marginally Controllable Expenses:		
Insurances (deductible/co-insurance)	$	$
Food		
Clothing		
Utilities (i.e., heat, a/c, water)		

Auto expenses including fuel		
Medical/Dental		
Other		
Other		
Total Marginally Controllable Exp.(C)	$	$
Debt Service:		
Credit card payments	$	$
Auto loan payments		
School loans		
Other		
Other		
Total Debt Service (D)	$	$
Taxes:		
Federal Withholding Tax + Return liability	$	$
FICA and Medicare		

State Withholding + Return liability		
Other taxes withheld or paid		
Total Taxes withheld and paid (E)	$	$
Voluntary Payments:		

Retirement Plan contributions	$	$
Charity		
Other		
Other		
Total Voluntary Payments (F)	$	$
Add: B+C+D+E+F	$	$
Subtract from A - Available Balance	$	$
Completely Discretionary Spending:		
Entertainment	$	$
Vacations		
Lottery Tickets		
Cable TV		
Other		
Other		
Other		
Total Completely Discretionary	$	$
Surplus (Deficit) (subtract CDS from Available Balance)	$	$

List your monthly outflows under each category. If the amounts vary, use a reasonable estimate. If there are costs that come up annually or seasonally, cut the cost into a monthly amount. Total all four categories to a total monthly outflow amount.

Next: Subtract your income from your expenses. If there's money left over, otherwise known as a surplus, where is it? Have you captured it, or has it somehow slid through the cracks into unknown expenditure?

If you have a deficit, we're just going to have to be creative. There are two clear approaches: Throw your hands up and give up, deciding it's too difficult, too mentally straining, too many obstacles to achieve success. *OR* you can get creative and take a baby step in the right direction.

IIIIIIIIII

Beginning to "Eat the Elephant": Making Small, Easy Changes

How in the world do you eat an elephant? As the old joke goes: one bite at a time! Yes, my friends, we cannot take your lifelong habits and make them disappear with the blink of an eye. For those of you who have deduced that the Powerball is the best strategy for handling your money misery . . . as we say in New Jersey, "Fuggedaboudit!"

Here's a way to start on your new menu of elephant munching: Grab your Cash Flow Worksheet, adjust your lobster bib, and let's dig in!

Begin with your list of discretionary expenses. Remember: You are focusing on *your* values, need for security, and peace of mind (think significantly increased pillow factor here).

What can you eliminate?

What costs can you shave back and by how much?

Total those costs and set up an automatic transfer from your checking account to a savings or separate account that you will use for debt elimination, asset accumulation, or another goal that equates with your financial *musts*.

That was easy, no fuss, no muss, no mass destruction, and very little in the way of pain and suffering. You've just made some pretty easy decisions to move closer to your values. In essence you are saying, "I value being debt-free more than I value eating out three times a week."

Think of it this way: We make choices every day. A lot of our decisions are based on convenience and lack of focus on our values. We employ the "it's only . . ." rationalization. Example: Buying paper towels at the organic market, rather than the discount store. We might value the organic produce and fish at the organic market, but paper towels might be significantly more money there than at the discount store. But because you are already *at* the organic market, we rationalize "it's only" this amount of money and the cost of gas to drive the 3.7 miles will *more* than make up for the difference in price. Right? Exactly! Except no—you're just being lazy.

We do what is convenient rather than what is in our best interest. Internet shopping has aided significantly to the overspending problem. An e-mail appears in your Inbox with all the specials and offers that are exactly what you want, need, and must have. *Click*—it's yours.

If you are receiving daily e-mails from your favorite site, unsubscribe, turn them off, and stop inviting temptation. It's like eating an arsenic-laced chocolate chip cookie because, well, it's on sale and you do love chocolate chip cookies.

There are so many small and easy steps you can take to help you on your quest to live the life of security and financial satisfaction. Each small shift is a conscious decision, rather than being constantly nudged by e-mails, commercials, people you know who want "company" in their habits, newspapers, television, movies, magazines, billboards, you name it. Wherever someone has the opportunity to tempt you, from the Audis prominently displayed in the *Ironman* movies to the ads on your computer home page. It's a constant stream of commercially fueled temptation to part you from your money and move your further from your dreams.

Continuing the Meal: Making More Difficult (but Necessary) Changes

I feel you tugging at my sweater, telling me that those discretionary expenses are just not enough to move the needle. Yes, of course, for many people, eating out one less night a week is not going to do it. We need to drill down to the next level. We need to examine the expenses that are marginally discretionary.

This is where some work is necessary. For example, your insurance policies might have very low deductibles and unnecessary benefits. You might have been talked into an expensive whole life insurance policy, or you might be keeping your thermostat too high or too low, depending on your geography and season. Each change results in a potential cost saving benefit. ***Note:*** If you change the deductible on your homeowner's policy from $250 to $2,500, make sure you have that $2,500 reserved in case of a claim. Find an independent agent who can help assess your current policies and where you can make changes that save money without taking imprudent risk.

Activating Your Moment of Truth When Small Changes Aren't Enough

Okay, you've cut back on your discretionary costs and saved money on the controllable costs (where you buy your groceries, clothes, etc.), and you've done a spectacular job of capturing the savings and putting them toward your primary goal and it is still not enough. What then? Well, that's where the moment of truth comes into play.

We all have moments of truth at various times in our lives. Deciding to get married, raise a family, take a job, quit a job—all are moments of truth. If you can find a way to close the gap by working an extra job, by all means, you won't be the first person on the planet to work a second job, and it might just be temporary until the crisis has passed. You are making huge strides in working toward your definition of success.

But what if it is still not enough? This is where we need to find all the strength and determination we can muster. Not because we happily make these choices, but because they are necessary. You might need to attack the fixed expenses, which means a "structural change." This means that the fixed expenses need to be altered so that your monthly burden is reduced. A structural change is a nice way of saying you might need to sell your home and move. You might need to rent someplace where the costs are less until you have the financial underpinning to do it comfortably.

There is no shame in having to make these changes. It happens. You've heard the expression, "Sometimes you have to take a step backwards to move forward." But, hey, reality check: You are where you are and more than likely it didn't happen without your involvement, and it's not going to improve without your involvement, either.

Sometimes, it is a result of our own less-than-enlightened decisions; other times, it is an offshoot of an uncontrollable situation (e.g., job loss, sickness or death in the family). The real shame is in the constant suffering you experience trying to navigate a situation that is centered on pain. Remember: You didn't knowingly take on your money mindset (discussed in Chapter 6). You became who you are—your beliefs, behaviors, and habits—as a result of your experience; what you saw through very young eyes. You did not purposefully adopt destructive habits.

But that doesn't mean you have to carry them on to your dying day and pass them on to your children. It *is* a choice. It's just not easy, until you have the time, space, and mindset to create new, more supportive habits. You have to believe that it rises above the level of "it would be nice if . . ." to "it *must* happen." Only then can you begin to creatively shape new possibilities.

You need to activate your creativity and desire to break bad habits, become more mindful of the decisions you make (life by design), keep your focus on your values, and get excited in creating a spectacular life. In Thomas Stanley's book *The Millionaire Next Door*, he talks about the successful person who has built a life of financial security. These successful people put greater value in their peace of mind than in the watch on their wrist. They don't require the trappings to prove their success to anyone. They are secure in the knowledge that they are okay and they will not be sucked into spending money on things that hold little value.

As you commune with your inner artist, know you are creating this work of art for you, your family, your core values, and future generations. Your daily meal of elephant will become tastier and tastier as you get accustomed to the change in diet. Your creativity and flare will add the necessary spices and flavors to make it work.

Bon appetit.

CHAPTER 8

Stoking Your Money Mojo

Mojo. According to *Merriam-Webster Dictionary*, mojo is "a power that may seem magical and that allows someone to be very effective, successful, etc."

You need your money mojo to be cranking on all cylinders to bring you out of a state of self-destruction and into a state of self-confidence and self-actualization. (Remember our old friend Maslow from Chapter 3?) Self-actualization entails living fully using your potential.

Finding your money mojo (aka your values mojo) is all about momentum. It's like changing your life by eating better or exercising more. Going to the gym and eating salads after a lifetime of burgers and fries is a shift of monumental proportion, and your brain will provide you with *every* reason why sitting on the couch with the grease dripping down your chin is a superior choice to the Stairmaster. It's the same voice that hits the snooze alarm and chirps that you really need, deserve, and must have those designer jeans regardless of the price.

So what can you do to defeat that little bugger that will pave your road with excuses and rationalization, and pretty much tell you that you can do anything you wish, consequences be damned? I could lie to you and tell you that it's easy and everything will be just fine—thank you very much. But the cold, hard, miserable fact is, as we've discussed, pain is involved. Have you ever worked out after being a bit stationary, and 18 hours later you feel like something big (like an elephant) just ran you over? That pain is real. But believe it or not, it is a good pain—a pain of progress and of something positive happening. Your previously unused muscles are being awakened, and blood is rushing to the assaulted areas to provide healing.

In this chapter, you will explore and create a money workout routine—something to follow consistently and by design. You will look at some old, weatherworn, and unusable beliefs, and replace them with shiny, new ones. Doesn't that sound like fun? You will also develop your "money code" and then talk about some ideas to support your efforts. Before you dive into your workout, time to stretch and take a good few breaths! Onward—strongly.

Starting a Money Workout Routine

Your money workout, like any prudent exercise plan, contains various levels of intensity and speed. Creating these money shifts, just like in any endeavor, requires the right mental attitude. It starts between your ears and extends outward. We know, without question, it is our mind that contains the memories, thoughts, beliefs, behaviors, and habits that we carry. The challenge is, like a Windows operating systems, it happens on an invisible level. We turn on the computer and the programs necessary do their thing. We don't see them, but we know they exist.

Those of us with difficult money messages have settled into habits that, although our normal, do not serve us effectively. We need to create a new normal that provides a higher level of happiness and purpose than what we've been living with all these years. Worksheet 8-1 offers you a short exercise to record old beliefs and replace them with something more affirming.

WORKSHEET 8-1: SHAPING UP OLD BELIEFS

Use this worksheet to write down your old beliefs about your money life, and replace them with something more positive and that you can work to achieve. I've provided an example to help get you started. Feel free to go back to Worksheet 1-1 to refresh yourself on some of your past observations—no need to re-create the wheel. You want to build messages that empower, strengthen, support, and reinforce your new money mojo.

Old Message	New Message
I spend money when I feel anxious. I rarely consider the impact on my cash flow.	I focus my spending on what I truly value and do not have the need to spend frivolously.

Change must start in the mind and flow outward—right to the fingertips that reach for the credit card.

What Would the New You Do?

Back to the workout. ***Old you:*** feels down or depressed, retail therapy sure to pick you right up. ***New you:*** gets up and goes for a walk, meets a friend for coffee, or does something creative or useful that doesn't entail a trip to the mall, store, or anywhere where the temptation exists. You have created an intentional path to break up old habits with new patterns that support your heart-driven goals. You will find that within a short period of time, the ache to shop or spend mindlessly has left, replaced by a different experience.

Now, the workout continues.

If you had gone to the store, your old pattern would have cost you a certain amount of money. What's the average? $20? $50?

Now, combining thought with action: Send that amount to your credit card company, savings, or investment account. With the advent of online banking and apps like Capital One 360, ImpulseSave, and SavingsPlus, it's right on your phone. Go ahead—sign on and get those funds out of your checking account, and apply them to your goals. Not only did you not add to the misery, but you took an active step to repair the damage and to improve your situation. Now think, decide, act, repeat!

You didn't even need to pay for a gym membership for this workout. But the benefits have lifelong implications. Can you feel your money mojo working?

We need our own code that guides our lives and improves our money mojo. The code spells out our purpose—purposefully, our reason to get up in the morning, and what allows us to put our heads on the pillow at night. We need this for our sanity, our happiness, our children, and future generations.

Worksheet 8-2 gives you an opportunity to create your own money code. As you create your money code, make it really meaningful. Write down a code that represents the life you deserve and the life you wish your children to have. Certainly, there is not a parent alive who wishes misery for their children, but misery exists because parents don't realize the implications of their actions and aren't prepared to talk about money in a meaningful way.

WORKSHEET 8-2: YOUR MONEY CODE

Your money code is your statement of who you are and what you believe when it comes to your financial life. It is your guide, foundation, and meaning.

Consider the following example and then create your own money code.

I will:

1. *Strive to live consistently with my stated values.*

2. *Strive to maintain a high level of focus on making decisions that align with my purpose.*

3. *Continue to learn more about financial matters that impact me and my family.*

4. *Accept and provide information to the stakeholders who are integral to my journey.*

5. *Honor the agreements I have made with myself and others.*

6. *Devote the time necessary to thoroughly evaluate the issues that need to be addressed to aid in my highest purpose.*

Getting the Help You Need: Finding a Trainer

If someone has no history of handling money properly or of making changes in their money approach, it's time to find a model, coach, or mentor. Let's face it: Some people are hard-wired to do things better than others. Whether they are athletes, musicians, builders, or doctors, they possess a certain innate ability to bring their skills and abilities to a finely honed level. But that doesn't assure them the skills to handle challenges outside their specialties.

I am one of those people who, no matter how many years I go to the gym, will never remember whether my hands need to grip the bar six inches apart, shoulder-width apart, or farther apart when doing certain exercises. I forget how many pounds to set the machine for or where my feet should be positioned. I am just lousy at it. That's why I have a trainer who reminds me about perfect positioning for each exercise and makes sure that I do 15 reps, not 13 or 14.

If money behavior is a problem, there are multiple choices to help you create useful and positive habits. Books like *Mind Over Money* by Brad and Ted Klontz and *Financial Recovery* by Karen McCall come to mind as examples of putting money and your values on the same page. Consider finding a qualified and experienced behavioral therapist who can help you model workable and satisfying habits. What about friends or family members who have successfully navigated their money lives? Can you get beyond your emotionally charged shame to ask them questions about how they found their money mojo?

Our society puts walls around the idea of talking about money. The mere mention raises defenses and evokes a defensive posture. We need to reject these ideas and create meaningful conversation and discussion, and it needs to start *early*. One of my favorite resources is Ron Lieber's book *The Opposite of Spoiled: Raising Kids Who Are Grounded, Generous and Smart About Money*. This should be required reading for everyone, as it counters the idea that money is a secret, not to be discussed and if spoken, only in hushed tones and not to be repeated under penalty of death. In other words, let's demystify the conversation and *get real!*

Is All This Work Really Worth It?

The reality is, if you haven't been able to do it by yourself up to now, the chances are you are going to need help to make this pivot. There's no crime or shame in asking for help—only in repeating behaviors that you **know** are destructive and broken.

If you have doubts, consider a "what if?" scenario. What's a "what if?" scenario, you ask? I'm glad you asked.

Ask yourself, "What if I continue doing what I am doing without change? What will my life be like 10, 20, or 30 years from now?"

Then ask yourself, "What could my life be like if I make slow and steady progress toward a better life? What will my life look like 10, 20, or 30 years from now?"

You see, we need to build a perspective that is far enough in the future because our actions today, though they feel small, like a little retail therapy that takes $20 or $30 out of your pocket, over time amount to an enormous amount of money. On top of that, think about all the interest charges you're paying. The $20 or $30 purchase could cost you hundreds of dollars by the time you finish paying it off.

Think about that $20 dollars per week, invested over 10, 20, or 30 years, earning a 6-percent rate of return (compounded annually). Ready? After 10 years, your $20 per week would be approximately $14,500; after 20 years, $40,550; and after 30 years, $87,150. That's opposed to spending $20 on your credit card with anywhere from 13- to 20-percent interest charges. It's a powerful message. One positive action brings you closer to your values, the other measurably farther away.

||||||||||

So, are you excited, pumped, and ready to move forward? Can you imagine how it feels to have security and choices? Can you see in your mind's eye how changing your beliefs about money can lead to positive habits, and a strong well-defined pathway from your present to a better future? You have created your money code, you have resources available, and you have the power and the ability. It's all goes into creating and maintaining your money mojo!

CHAPTER 9

Tame Blame and Shame: A Ramp to Resilience

The interesting thing about being human is our ability to screw up, fall back to old habits, and fail. But that's what makes us so spectacular. We can get back up and do some serious loin girding. (Note to reader: I threw that in because it makes me laugh. I remember hearing the expression "girding your loins" when I was a kid and it always cracked me up. Even after I figured out what it meant, it still made me laugh. Welcome to my sense of humor.) Our innate ability to hit the reset button and start again allows us to find our inner strength and the determination to reach our goals.

Expected and unexpected transitions in our lives are normal. Those who are resilient are better equipped to navigate changes, bounce back from disappointments, and welcome new opportunities with openness and a positive outlook.

It all sounds good in words, but getting through transitions successfully requires a tool kit of practical skills, money mojo, and the ability to get through the challenges.

In this chapter, we will talk about the importance of becoming financially resilient. You'll begin to build your resilience muscle and look at some examples of resilient people. In addition, we will look at some ideas that will put you back on track after missteps. Many people live in shame of their situation and project those feelings as blame toward self and others. We know that is a formula for continued misery, and by now you know quite clearly this journey is all about celebrating successes, honoring our humanness, and living a life that aligns with our highest values.

Blame and Shame: On the Highway to Hell

"I feel so stupid."

"How did I let it get this bad?"

"I am such a failure."

"If only I got that raise. . . ."

"I told him that he needed to pay attention to our finances!"

Blame. Self-blame. Blaming others. Each form of blame is just a misplaced cry resulting from a lack of understanding, training, and foundational money knowledge. Some of us are "avoiders" and others are "worriers." Worriers devote countless hours to flawed logic and magical thinking. Avoiders distract themselves with "if only" and "what if?" thinking. Both lead ultimately to blame and shame.

But let's stop and think about this from another perspective. Avoiding something that is beyond your knowledge, comfort, understanding, and interest is the fertilizer in the soil in which money dysfunction thrives. Why do we avoid? My best guess is there is more pain involved with getting down in the dirt and dealing with it than in avoiding, leaning on the fantasy that it will all be ok. And that might work, at least for a time.

We feel shame when we compare ourselves to others in our circle or up against the image of where we *should* be. Consider the following example.

||||||||||

Andrea and Tom sat next to each other in the meeting room. Andrea began, "I don't even know what to say. Tom said he had this all handled, and here we are: credit card debts, owing the IRS, and our daughter is graduating from high school next year. How did this happen?"

Tom shot back, "Every time I tried to talk to you about our money, you were too busy. Do you remember saying 'Listen, I am up to capacity with running the kids here and there. There's just no time.'? Do you remember? You can blame me all you want, but I did try several times to bring you into the problems."

Andrea's tone was less than angry, "You should have been more specific and insisted. We didn't need to go on that vacation with the kids, and you certainly didn't need the new golf clubs and lessons."

Tom retorted, "Just as you didn't need to be a member of the club or buy all those clothes . . . and—"

I cut him off. "Excuse me, but can you help me understand how this is helping other than to further poison an already toxic soup? You're here to get your life back on track. How is all this blame helping?"

Andrea, looking down, murmured, "I feel so ashamed. How do we fix this?"

|||||||||||

These conversations are all too common. The reality is that we look outward before we peer inward. We try to portray a view for the world to adore and admire even if we are living a lie. There's a phrase in Latin, which resonated deeply: *ab intra*, meaning "from within." That's where it must start. That's where it all must start, with a deep-seated need and desire to make changes that you know in advance will shatter your comfort zone. The good news is, building a new comfort zone, one step at a time, is glorious work. Resilience is that inner spark that pushes us to regroup and try again. Our resilience is the fuel that takes us to higher levels of competence and builds confidence that we can move forward to break through our resistance. The result is an "I can—I will—I *must*" attitude that further supports your long-term success.

Bouncing Back: The Importance of Becoming Financially Resilient

Most of life's transitions have a financial connection; therefore it is necessary to think about ways to strengthen your ability to be more financially and emotionally resilient. Your ability to understand your situation and the potential options and opportunities is a great place to start. Think about something you know thoroughly—I mean black-belt, "I got this" status. You have comfort navigating your way through, around, inside, and outside of this skill. In other words, you know it. If you were faced with a challenge concerning this area, you would know how to manage that situation.

When it comes to money, however, very few of us have that level of know-how. We've already discussed in Chapter 1 the importance of knowing your numbers. The more comfort and facility you have with understanding the dynamics of your numbers, the more comfort you will have in making decisions.

For example, I used to work with a nutritionist who told me, "You need to know the value of what you eat. If you have a 2,200-calorie allowance for the day and your spend 1,000 of them on KitKat bars, well, then you have 1,200 calories for the rest of the day. Your other option is to exercise and earn back calories so that you stay on target." You know what? It works. I learned to trade miles on the treadmill for a drink at dinner or some chocolate. It was a guilt-free experience. It's simple math, really: If I earn back 135 calories for every

mile on the treadmill and one cocktail is 140 calories
. . . you see?

Well, money and finances are really the same idea.
Your daily "calorie" allotment is a certain sum of money.
You get to choose how you wish to apportion your available "calories." My hope and wish is that your choices
are focused on the ones you value most. And unless you
are willing to make "structural" changes, such as selling
your home and moving into a less-expensive living environment, your fixed costs have to come first. (Refer to
Chapter 7 for more on fixed versus discretionary costs
and on making "structural" changes when necessary.)

"What does this have to do with resilience? Why are
you babbling about all this stuff I've already covered?"
you ask wisely. Well, there are times when I didn't jump
on the treadmill that day, and I had to make a decision
when dessert was offered. (Dark chocolate molten lava
cake with the dark chocolate ganache poured all over that
bad boy with homemade vanilla ice cream on the side. . . .
Sorry, I just got lost in the moment. Give me a second to
recover. Okay, I'm back. Thank you for your understanding.) I don't have the required space within my 2,200 calorie allotment, and I will have to deal with the reality of the
moment: *I want that cake!* My choices are to walk away
from the table and run out of the restaurant screaming,
order the dessert and eat a small amount so that I don't go
over my daily goal, or eat it all and bust the daily budget.

My brain is on fire, torn between desires. Intellectually,
I *know* I should take my own good advice and run screaming out into the dark night. I *know* I will be very proud

of myself later for resisting this amazing plate of absolute yumminess. But there's a part of my brain that is coaxing me to pick up the fork and soothe that emotional part that would be so happy—no, thrilled, delighted, fulfilled, and just a few miles south of nirvana—if I just go for it.

Well, as my friend Meg the nutritionist told me, "Hey, we all have bad days. The question is not whether we have a bad day; it's whether we allow that bad day to become a bad week, month, or year. Where do the brakes get applied to get you back on track?"

I guess you can see the parallel here. There will be times when there's a part of you that is bleeding for something that will soothe the part of you that is feeling denied, frustrated, angry, and needy. So what will you do? There is a huge difference between an occasional deviation and an all-out surrender. If your objective is clear and your values defined, then the only way from your current situation to success is your ability to make decisions that are aligned with your preferred outcomes—as consistently as possible.

Here are a few tips to think about:

1. Know your numbers and the flexibility in your spending plan. For instance, if you have $100 in your spending plan for entertainment, and nothing left in your clothing allotment, you can decide to eliminate the entertainment in lieu of something you value more. If your spending plan has a $200 utilities budget and your bill comes in at $162, you can shift the

difference to another category, debt payment, or savings.

2. Understand the impact of making a decision that takes you away from your mission. If the impact will create greater pain or loss, there's really only one answer.

3. Before deciding, stop long enough to have that inner conversation.

4. Think about what will prevent this decision from pushing you in the wrong direction. Lean on your support, your money billboards (from Chapter 5), and your values.

Your mission, the one you have created to find financial security, requires hard work, focus, and a real understanding of your values. Those lofty goals to change your habits, your outlook, and your life come at a cost. Remember that you didn't get to the place that created the lack of true fulfillment by accident. It was actions—your actions, based on the beliefs, behaviors, and habits that you owned and operated. You have ownership of your past actions and your present decisions; the difference is, you now have the tools and outlook to make better choices.

Building Your Emotional Strength to Be More Resilient

You failed. You gave in. You bailed on the plan you so carefully devised. You overspent on something that wasn't in the "buy" column. You experienced a moment of weakness, and now you are left with regret, internal castigation, and self-degradation. Feel better? Nah, probably not. Now what?

Financial resilience requires emotional strength and a degree of maturity. This is achieved by identifying the fears, and the behaviors triggered by those fears, and working to understand and overcome the whys of your actions; it's called taking responsibility.

One way to find emotional strength is to remember a time when you exhibited that strength successfully. It's like riding a bicycle: Once you learn how, you'll have it forever. So, when was the last time you used your inner strength to overcome an obstacle, challenge, or crisis? How did you do it? What was the outcome, and how did you feel about yourself with that accomplishment? If you've done it before, you can and must do it again.

Resilience is a trait or personal characteristic that you can nurture. In *Making Sense of Life's Transitions*, William Bridges wrote, "There are ways of facilitating transitions, and they begin with recognizing that letting go is at best an ambiguous experience. . . . They involve developing new skills for negotiating the perilous passage across the 'nowhere' that separates the old life situation from the new."

Armed with this knowledge, you know that the road is fraught with challenge, but you also acknowledge that you've mastered other skills in your life, experienced other problems, or faced difficulties and figured out how to navigate it successfully. It's important.

So, you screwed up. It's probably not fatal. Your decision might have led you off the road a bit, but there's an on-ramp right in front of you. Begin anew with a deeper understanding of the cause and effect of your decision so that you will be better prepared the next time you are faced with a challenge. Understand the facts and circumstances that put you in the position in the first place. How could you avoid this in the future? That's called learning, folks. It means turning off the cruise control and taking responsibility for driving the car.

Common Traits of Resilient People

Becoming resilient allows you to continuously add to your experience and build your skills to handle life and the wide swath of obstacles that litter the landscape. Being resilient makes you happy because it makes you *able* and empowered. It's like earning that black belt, that PhD, or the captaincy of your life's ship. You have control. What do resilient people have in common?

- They feel good about themselves, and their self-esteem is rarely affected by the criticism and negative opinions of others.
- They are emotionally stable and are not easily "rattled" in stressful situations.
- Even in difficult situations, they don't give up.
- They stay in control of the direction their lives are taking.

In the following worksheet, you will have the opportunity to consider your experience with resilience by recording some of your real-life examples. Have fun and don't forget to celebrate your incredible feats of resilience and strength!

WORKSHEET 9-1: WORKING ON YOUR RESILIENCE

There is a great deal written on the idea of using past successes to create a tie to new successes. If you were successful once, you know you have what it takes to create success in the future. For those who cannot recall a past success, talk to someone you know who has achieved success in something, and find out how they created the success and what obstacles they overcame to get there.

Try this exercise:

1. Record three or four examples of when you displayed resilience in your life.

2. Write down what you did, how you did it, and what challenges you experienced in creating that success. Create a detailed list of steps and obstacles.

3. Describe how you felt when you were successful.

Achieving Gradual Change Through Self-Awareness

Self-awareness is a key concept in what you're trying to accomplish. Asking yourself the important questions and being flat out honest with your answers. When building new skills and resilience it is vital that you have a clear understanding of your *whys*. As you become more aware, you start to realize that the old messages and experiences don't serve you well. That being said, it is not like turning off a light switch. You don't just turn off a lifetime of beliefs with the snap of your fingers. Change is a process that is no more a direct line from misery to ecstasy than did Thomas Edison wake up one morning and invent the light bulb on his first attempt.

I remember joining a gym and meeting with a trainer, after being very inactive for a long period of time. He tested me on a treadmill and got my heart rate up way too quickly. After a few minutes of rest, he checked my heart rate again and to my dismay, it hadn't changed from my elevated rate during activity. He looked at me and said, "This ain't good, dude." So my answer was to get a heart rate monitor and get my sorry ass on the treadmill, carefully checking as I brought my rate up and watched it go back down. It took time and patience to bring my fitness level up to a good level. But it didn't happen overnight, and it wasn't without efforts.

||||||||||

This chapter was packed with a great deal of information to unpack and consider. There was a lot to think about, recall, and dissect. Are you currently in a state of self-blame and shame? Can you see how blaming and shaming is a self-defensive posture that deflects the real issue, the real fear, and the real solutions? It is clear that there is so much emotion wrapped up around money and money issues that we need to find a path to a better state. The best weapon against this condition is to find the strength in resilience and look to examples of your own successes and those of others who have overcome great obstacles. I know you can.

I am sure you are wondering if I ate that amazing dark chocolate molten lava cake and dark chocolate ganache with homemade vanilla ice cream on the side. Right? Let me put it this way: I accomplished a new record for me by racking up eight miles on the treadmill the next day.

CHAPTER 10

The Tao of Financial Planning

It's easy to say that everyone should consider and prepare a financial plan that incorporates the basic needs of security and long-term financial happiness. What could be simpler in concept, yet more challenging to actually create?

You get the *whys*, right? Everyone wants to put their heads on the pillow knowing that they are on track to live their dreams, or at the very least to avoid disaster. Yet, we get stuck by our lack of basic financial knowledge to know the right questions to ask in our search for direction. This chapter provides some basic how-to information that will enable you to move in the right direction and gain insights into areas in which you have less comfort or understanding.

We all know that planning is about the future, whether you are taking a trip across the country or providing for retirement, sending children to college, or helping out a family member in time of need. In order to get to your ultimate destination, you need to consider what you need to do to get there. It's about choices and, frankly, the ordering of discomfort (pain). Giving up something you are accustomed to is painful. Living every day with collection notices, looming college tuition, or retirement around the corner is *real* pain, especially if it puts your very existence in jeopardy. The problem comes into focus when you are wrestling between today's pain and some future possibility that you know intellectually is out there, but you're just not feelin' it today. We are great maskers of reality (aka avoiders) and can come up with a self-justified excuse for something that our brain tells us we *neeeeeeeeeeed!* But, if you take a breath, take a walk, and take a moment to consider what is really going on, you will see that it's just the part of your personality (call it your inner child) that is picking away at your intellectual/knowing (mature) self.

A proper financial plan is all about harmony—where all the parts work together. Though there might not be 100-percent satisfaction in every area, enough consideration is given to ensure that your life goals are not decimated by ignoring something really important.

Know Your Numbers to Manage Cash Flow

Let's go back to your numbers. What's coming in the door and what's going out? Take the time to get into the details of your spending. Analyze each expense category and understand it. For example, when you look at your insurance costs, review your deductibles, policy limits, co-insurance, and riders. Think about each item and its importance to your overall objectives. Managing your cash flow is really important. You need to be able to react to changes that occur. For example, if the cost of gasoline goes down, the difference between what you typically spend and what it costs now needs to be captured. If you receive a rebate or savings from rewards programs, those amounts should be captured and saved. Although it might sound small, each step forward brings you closer to your desired goal. Each step reinforces the habits you need to be successful. Be prepared to use the fork-in-the-road approach for spending decisions. For those expenses that you just can't decide, take a more biblical approach: Try to cut the cost in half and see how that fits. You will find that the fear of cutting expenses is usually greater than the actual pain.

What happens if you decide that you just cannot make *any* changes to your discretionary pile? That's a big dilemma, as you cannot move closer to your values without making some choices. The reality is that you have not truly embraced your core values, and I suggest you go back to the chapter that helped you explore what's most important to you.

Time to put some meat on the bones (unless you're a vegetarian, in which case I give you permission to think of a more suitable metaphor).

The following worksheet is your opportunity to start putting the concepts we've been discussing together to help formulate some concrete steps. Embrace the opportunity to dig in and get really excited about your next steps.

WORKSHEET 10-1: TURNING YOUR MONEY PLAN INTO ACTION

You've done the work in understanding your numbers and, most of all, what beliefs, behaviors, and habits have supported actions that work against your values. You've made the efforts to think deeply about the life you want, deserve, and crave. You've considered what will increase your pillow factor to provide a feeling of support, security, and control.

Now it's time to work on a plan that will provide step-by-step guidance to move closer to your goals.

In a previous chapter, we discussed the idea of *musts.* Your *musts* are the stated values that will not or cannot be sacrificed. They simply *must* happen.

Examples: "In order to feel financially secure, I ***must*** *live without revolving debt." "In order to make sure I do not outlive my resources, I* ***must*** *accumulate enough resources to cover my needs throughout my expected lifetime."*

Given your imperatives, you can now make decisions that work in harmony with your objective. For example, "In order to live without revolving debt, I must alter my spending habits and focus on only those purchases that support my goal."

Now, the how-tos:

State Your Must(s):

Who are the stakeholders in your objectives?

Are they on board?

Do you know the difference between a need and a want?
Record your definitions here:

    Need:

    Want:

Past Successes

Recount a time when you accomplished your goal.

What was it?

How did you do it?

How did you feel when you achieved your desired goal?

What obstacles exist to prevent you from your next success?

The Numbers

Categories	Current Amount	Increases	Decreases	Revised Amount
Current Income				
Opportunities to Increase Income				
Total Available Income				
Fixed Expenses				
Is there a need to make structural changes?				
If so, what are the new fixed expenses after change?				
Partially Discretionary Spending				
What small shifts can you make?				
—Become more energy efficient				
—Shop for gas, clothing, medical care, RX, other commodities more efficiently				

Completely Discretionary				
What are you willing to do to reach your goals in areas you have the power to change (i.e., vacations, entertainment, gifts, etc.)?				
Income Tax (dependent on your taxable income)				
Your New Spending Plan Surplus				

Now that you can see where you can make shifts in your thinking and actions, you want to start taking those changes and channeling them toward your *musts*.

If your *must* is getting out of debt, then every shift or change that results in a savings should be actively applied against those balances. Start with the highest interest rate debt and work your way down. Make daily payments if you're achieving daily savings. Online banking makes this simple. If you decide not to spend $100 from a budget item, send that $100 right to the credit card company.

The same goes for accumulation goals. It's as simple as transferring dollars from account A to account B. Here's the bonus: Every time you *add* to your accumulation or *lessen* your debt, the emotional rush of satisfaction is wonderful. There is a cause for celebration and appreciation for every action that shifts your thinking from thoughtless routine to a mindful choice. Each victory is a huge step forward.

Continually Review Spending and Saving Habits

Review your spending and savings habits. How often do you actively save, and what percentage of your income is being captured? Are you a free spender, or do you make prudent decisions and consider the impact of spending before you slap down your credit card? Remember our discussion about our lives being over-committed? Well, in order to make good decisions, you must have the time and attention necessary to do so. I suggest creating a set time during the week to talk about money, make decisions, and assess your progress. There's everything right about the question: So how did we do this week?

The real question is your level of connection to your financial life. Remember: If you don't feel comfortable dealing with financial matters, you will most likely avoid it like the Ebola virus. We all have areas about which our discomfort causes us to run and hide. I'm like that with anything mechanical. When it comes to anything that goes wrong or breaks in the house, I defer to my wife to deal with because I know it makes me break out in hives. I also know and acknowledge that her organizational skills and attention to detail make her much better at dealing with contractors and repairmen (whereas I zone out to complete inattentiveness).

We all have areas that create heightened anxiety and mental shutdown. Sometimes, it's necessary to change the time, location, or approach of the conversation. When things get tense, it's best to disengage, take a walk, go for a run, practice yoga, and then come back after the anxiety has passed and you're able to start over. On the other hand, the results of your continued disengagement from your financial life carry with them consequences of epic proportion: your life.

Think About Short-Term, Mid-Range, and Long-Term Goals

Outline your goals using a timeline (time until college, retirement, purchase of a new car, etc.). Create a resource allocation based on time and importance. Use color coding for short-term (zero to three years), mid-range (four to seven years) and long-term (eight years or more). Color coding helps you identify and separate your goals and keep your focus on where the attention needs to be. Okay, so I stole the idea from the commercial about "orange" money, but it makes sense. Make your goals stand out. Put them in flashing neon envelopes if it helps.

Manage Your Risk

When reviewing your investments, think risk. Investing in stocks is appropriate when you have sufficient time to withstand market downturns. Stock market investments are never appropriate for short-term goals. If you are planning on buying a new car in three years and stick your car money into the stock market, thinking you are going to get great returns—think again. You might—but your down payment might get decimated by a down year or two, making the purchase impossible.

You might have heard terms like *diversification* and *allocation*. Simply put, diversification is making sure your investments are in many different companies, thus spreading the risk. If you buy mutual funds that are actively managed, you might be shocked to find out that although each fund might have anywhere from 30 to 3,000 different stocks in them, when you look inside the different funds you own, you might find that each fund buys many of the same companies. Therefore, your portfolio is not as diversified as you might believe.

Allocation refers to how you portion the types of investments between different areas or asset classes, such as stocks versus bonds, large company versus small, foreign versus domestic, growth versus value. Your allocation will help determine how much risk you are accepting in your portfolio.

Investing is another one of those areas in which the hype is overwhelming. Forget the Wall Street insanity and overinflated promises. Look for low cost index-type funds and keep more money in your pocket. The hype will most likely lead you into making emotional and ill-conceived decisions.

Another word about investing: It's a long-term project, and judging success is more about how your portfolio stacks up to its benchmarks than the highest performing asset class, stock, or fund. Chasing returns is a sucker's game and a loser's game. Grab a copy of Charles Ellis's book *Winning the Losers' Game*, or *The Investment Answer* by Gordon Murray and Daniel Goldie for a primer of sensible investing. The idea that just because a particular fund or stock did well last year, it will continue to do so into the future is ridiculous. Here's a typical story: A small, maybe relatively unknown mutual fund screams to the top of the performance charts and now becomes really well known, as the financial press praise it up to the heavens. What starts out as a small, well-managed fund where the manager finds appropriate investments based on the size and scope of the fund, turns into a dog the next year. All the attention creates a flood of money into the fund. So here's the "poor" manager sitting with a ton of cash that needs to be put somewhere, because no one is paying sizeable fees to sit in cash. He has to now go out and find nooks and crannies to stick all this money. The selection process has now been replaced by wholesale "gotta get this cash put to work" mode. What do you think the chances of this manager duplicating the past performance? (Hint: not good!)

Allocate Resources to Your Goals

Allocate your resources actively to your goals. Whether you are paying down debt or accumulating assets, your active participation in making these decisions is vital. Review your surplus (what's left over after expenses) and apply the funds to the areas of your financial life that are most important and pressing. This needs to be done every time you receive income or actively create a saving. Remember the old axiom (that I just made up) "Nothing good can happen when you leave surplus funds in your checking account." The more frequently you are actively working on your goals, the more quickly these actions become good habits and then a part of you and your mission. There isn't an amount too small to be applied in pursuit of your dreams. A lack of action can very easily lead back to old habits that invariably move you in the opposite direction of where you need to be. Once you are moving forward, don't let the momentum slow down.

Take a Proactive Approach with Taxes

Do you wind up with a windfall tax refund or paying a ton each year? Do you wind up paying penalties and interest? If so, tax management is something requiring your attention. Unless your tax situation is completely basic, then spend the money and work with a CPA who can guide you—proactively.

Tax awareness is important. For example, knowing your marginal bracket, what is deductible, and what can and should be accelerated, deferred, delayed, or avoided (not as in tax evasion, but avoidance of specific strategies or tax decisions) is important information. The IRS has a lot of good information (irs.gov) that is fairly understandable.

There are basic tenets of taxes that will smooth your cash flow and aid you in making wise decisions. For example, if you are planning on taking profits from an investment, make sure you have held it for one year and a day before selling to qualify for long-term capital gains treatment. Though that strategy from a tax point of view makes all the sense in the world, make sure you consider the economics as well. For example, if you experience a substantial gain and it is significantly less than a year and you are ill-disposed to gamble the loss of the profit, consider a stop loss order on the account so that you will not watch your profits disappear. In assessing your true profit, you have to account for the tax cost, whether long term (favorable rate) or short term (ordinary income rates). If you are working with a stock broker, understand that they are very happy if you do well, but they do not have a fiduciary responsibility to act in your best interest. Make sure you ask questions and get complete, understandable, and relevant answers. Buying and selling creates taxable events, and also adds commissions into the brokers' pocket.

Have a Plan for Your Estate

Do you have a signed and properly executed will? If you have dependents, then there's no better way to say, "I don't care about you!" more than **not** having appropriate documents. I don't know about you, but I don't want the state deciding anything—especially how and who will take care of my children. Without a will, the law of intestacy falls to state law. Good luck with that! Other important documents include powers of attorney, which provides the mechanism for someone to act on your behalf for financial matters, if you are unable to do so for yourself. Is this important? Only if you're disabled—and then it's *really* important.

Estate planning allows for an orderly disposition or transfer of your estate to your beneficiaries. Settling an estate, even if it is relatively simple is, at best, a headache and, at worst, a complete disaster. Litigation over estate disposition is becoming increasingly common, unfortunately. The best way to avoid these disasters is to have a family who talks with each other and shares information openly. There's a relatively new movement called collaborative estate planning that brings together several disciplines (attorney, planner, social worker) to conduct family meetings. There are other areas of estate planning that indeed require your attention, such as having a child with special needs, assets that need liability protection, or an elderly relative who is in danger of being left destitute during their final years. These are just a few of the areas regarding estate planning that need attention and consideration in your overall planning.

Be Realistic About Retirement

Savings for retirement is a bear. Why? Well, first of all, you don't know how long you're going to live and what it will cost to live when your income-earning days are over.

Check your social security account annually; make sure it's correct. You only have a small window to correct mistakes. (Can you believe the government makes mistakes?) Use the Social Security Administration Website (ssa.gov) to set up and access your account.

Think of savings for retirement like a paycheck-to-paycheck bill that needs to get paid: little by little, but steadily. Make sure you increase your retirement plan contributions whenever your salary increases. If you're in your 30s or 40s, you may have no idea what you want your retirement life to look like. You probably know that at some point you'd like to slow down and, even if you love what you do, you will have to stop at some point. So what are you waiting for?

The old definition of retirement was something like this: Retire at 65, collect Social Security for a few years, and die. (At least that was how the government had it figured.) That image of retirement has been reshaped by the imagination of the retiree. Retirement can mean a second career, further education, more leisure, more adventure, more activity, more volunteering, more political involvement, more babysitting for the grandkids, and more exploration. This means you need a bigger nest egg to last you more years of vibrant living. There have been many studies focused on retirement that points to the need for increased physical, mental, social activity, and the promotion of more meaning in life. Here's the caveat: It's pretty much not free. If I've learned anything in more than 30 years in this business, it is that what people want in life is *more options*. Therefore, the more options you want, the more money you have to have. Or as our friends the ancient Romans said, *"Res ipsa loquitur!"* Right?

Learn to Have Peaceful, Productive Conversations About Money

In order to reach accord on money issues, it's essential that all stakeholders work together, bonded by common goals. This makes changes easier and more directed. When was the last time you had an actual conversation about money that was comfortable, meaningful, and helped bring you closer by talking about shared values? Try having a conversation that is safe and without blame, and that focuses on your values, concerns, and goals.

The following worksheet is a guide to having money conversations that are productive and supportive.

WORKSHEET 10-2: MONEY CONVERSATIONS

Here's a process to follow to get you through money conversations:

1. **Leave blame, shame, insecurity, and lack of knowledge at the door.** The idea is to create understanding by asking questions that begin with "Help me understand. . . ." Once an explanation is furnished, there is no argument, debate, or analysis.

2. **Make a list of the agreed-upon areas for discussion.** Because money is such a sensitive topic, leave the grisly ones for later; start small and easy. For example, if you know your partner is very sensitive about a particular area of spending (say, the deluxe cable package or expensive hair and nail treatments), put it on the sideline until trust is established and defensive barriers are lowered. Instead, start out with something like:

   - "How can we co-create our big-picture goals?"
   - "What seems to be the biggest issue weighing on you?"
   - "How can we work together to make good decisions?" (It's always better to ask and not tell.)
   - "What do you think we can each do to move us closer to our biggest, most important goals?"

- "Will you help me when I get frustrated or off target by gently reminding me?"
- "How can I help you when you get frustrated or off target?

3. **Once you've made your list of what to tackle first, approach the issue as if you were not involved.** Try to remain dispassionate. *Examples: "The cheaper gas station is two blocks farther but is less costly. Can we agree to go a little bit out of our way to use that station while it's financially advantageous?" "Dry Cleaner A charges $.99 per shirt, and our regular dry cleaner charges $2.00. Can we agree to try Dry Cleaner A to test out whether they do a good enough job?"*

4. **Do the math as you go.** $.06 per gallon times 15 gallons times two fill-ups per week per car—that's almost $200 per year. Five shirts per week times $1.01 times 50 weeks is more than $250 per year. Sounds small? Those two areas of savings per year over 20 years earning 6 percent is approximately $10,000. Would you prefer that *ten thousand dollars* in your pocket?

5. **As you get better at finding creative ways to making financial changes, you will inevitably bump into resistance.** At this point, it's time to go back to the *whys* and understanding. Many times, the resistance is because of some deep-seated belief or fear. *Examples: "If I don't have this, others will*

think I am poor." "It makes me feel bad if I cannot do that." These are pretty strong emotions that might require help from a qualified therapist. Therapy can be a very worthy investment in your future success and your present happiness. If your progress is halted because of those inner voices, outside help can help you create steps to reinforce your beliefs.

6. **Accept the fact that you're never done.** Your vigilance and attention are required to get you to your destination. If you're the airline pilot flying from New York to Los Angeles, you just don't quit over Kansas. Your mantra of "Nothing is more important than _____" will help get you through the rough spots.

Seek the Help You Need

Financial planning is not magic, mysterious, or untethered from other human activities, but is has a lot of moving parts. Knowing what you can do for yourself and what you need help with is really important. Wasting time on areas where real objective expertise and experience is necessary is tantamount to looking up do-it-yourself brain surgery on WebMD. Buy the help when appropriate; it is far cheaper than floundering around trying to cobble together bits and pieces of data without real knowledge and applying it to something as important as your future. Remember my experience in auto maintenance?

There is help out there. You can hire a fee-only financial planner to help you deal with the technical issues and get you on track. You can source a local planner through the National Association of Personal Financial Advisors website (NAPFA.org) or the Financial Planning Association Website (www.onefpa.org). You might hire someone who works hourly or on a retainer basis, depending on your need and resources. Always ask, in advance, how they are compensated, whether they have any conflicts of interest, and be sure they hand you their ADV disclosure document. Beware of any "advisor" who offers to do planning for free in exchange for managing your money. You might also have the need of a qualified CPA, in which case the American Institute of Certified Public Accountants (www.AICPA.org) has resources, along with the local CPA Society. Always ask up-front about costs, charges, and conflicts of interest. Though a local tax shop might be fine for simple returns, these are not high-level tax professionals. There are CPAs who will prepare your taxes and then offer to invest your money. Best to avoid these obvious conflicts.

When it comes to getting wills and estate documents prepared, I strongly urge you not to go online and pull off a document that might or might not suffice. Make sure the person you work with is an expert in this area and not someone who does real estate closings or divorce work as their primary focus. The ramifications of a mistake are too dear to mess around. There are several resources to find the right estate planning attorney, including the American Bar Association (www.american bar.org), the American College of Estate & Trust Counsel (www.actec.org), the National Association of Estate Planners and Councils (www.naepc.org), and the American Academy of Estate Planning Attorneys (www .aaepa.com). All organizations can lead you to a local practitioner.

|||||||||||

You've done great work here. There was an awful lot to consider and digest. You have the tools to make good decisions and begin to move forward strongly to live your values and achieve your *musts*. After all, if it *must* happen, only you can make it happen—because you care *that* much. Don't allow the "now monster" that confuses needs and wants from pulling you down the wrong path. I know you can do it, and most of all, **you** know you can, too.

CHAPTER 11

Living Intentionally to Live Richly

Way back in Chapter 6, we talked about Benjamin Franklin and his system to work actively on his values as a precursor for Worksheet 6-1. If you've never heard the story of Benjamin Franklin's great success, he started off at age 17 mired in debt, but subsequently retired at age 42 a very wealthy man. It is a story for the ages—the classic rags to riches, but with an underpinning of values—or, as he put it, "principles" and practical rules for living that became habits. He devoted each week to cultivating and focusing on each of the 13 principles, thereby working on each four weeks per year, every year. The idea is that success requires active efforts centered on values. (Refer back to Chapter 6 for his list and review your worksheet before proceeding.)

In this chapter, we will focus on ideas and actions that prompt self-awareness and intentional behavior, which lead to positive empowering habits. You will have the opportunity to examine your current habits that lead to unwanted outcomes and consider what actions can replace them to lead you to live the values you so deeply want.

Turning Off Autopilot and Developing Self-Awareness

Whether you endeavor to adopt Ben's habits of focusing each week on another principle or not, having a set of rules, beliefs, practices, or virtues that become the foundation of your values is really important. These beliefs or practices become the solid bedrock on which you build your life. Problems occur when our lives are so unfocused and out of control, distracted by the daily noise, that we forget what's really important.

You might scoff at the idea and justify your lack of focus on the weather, the Internet, Obamacare, or your kid's soccer schedule, but honestly, those are pretty much lame excuses. The reality is we get stuck in a rut of habit, supported by our beliefs, by our laziness, by our confusion or lethargy. Let's remember: Habits can be helpful and supportive or destructive and negative.

In order to understand your habits, a heaping portion of active awareness must be ingested. Here's where you get to do some work.

WORKSHEET 11-1: BRINGING AWARENESS TO YOUR HABITS

Make a list of your routine: what you do, when you do it, and why.

Habit	Time of Day	Why
Brush my teeth	First thing in the AM	I believe in good personal hygiene.
Grocery shopping	During lunch	It's the most convenient time.

Get the idea?

Now, assess whether these habits work or whether changes are beneficial.

I don't mind grocery shopping; however, I know that if I shop without a list, I am either going to buy things I don't need or forget something. If I go when I am hungry, the chances are my cart will be filled with items that tempt my palate—not necessarily what I need. Creating mindfulness around something as mundane as doing your weekly shopping can lead to effective self-management. You have the opportunity to be efficient, save money by use of coupons, and picking the most effective place to purchase specific items. You remember all that creativity we talked about? Set your inner artist free to find creative ways to make great choices and expand your options.

Great habits will smooth your trek to success, whereas lousy habits can almost assure you of maximum strife and struggle, if not failure. The exception to the latter is, of course, if you have more money than you could ever spend, then your bad habits won't sink your ship. (But then again, if you have more money than you could ever spend, you probably didn't buy this book anyway, unless you just bought it to be nice to me—in which case, thank you!)

Having a routine is comforting; while providing a sense of control, it is really just the illusion of control. However, if the routine or set of habits adds to your misery, a serious revisit is in order. There are some great books out there that can help you onto a path of mindfulness, such as *Mindfulness for Beginners* by Jon Kabat-Zinn and *The Art of Power* by Thich Nhat Hahn.

As you assemble your list of new supportive habits, remember to make it as complete as possible. Infuse mindfulness and prompts to help you stay in a mindful mode. Don't leave anything off, from the beginning of the day to the end. It is important to examine, evaluate, and understand each habit and how it is either additive to your success or destructive.

Avoiding Common Destructive Habits

Following are some common habits that are sure to push you backward financially:

1. Feeling stressed. You hit the mall and start filling up your basket. The habit of retail therapy is sure to add to the problem.

2. Not knowing what costs what. With the availability of information, there's simply no excuse not to comparison shop.

3. Spending dollars on items of little value. Here's the classic "convenience over conviction": Stopping to fill up the tank at the closest gas station, rather than the cheapest, just because it's a block or two out of the way. Another one is buying the extended warranty on low-cost items just because all you have to do is "click" the box rather than question or do the research whether it makes any sense at all. Service contracts and extended warrantees are financial boons for providers, but they are mostly a waste of your hard-earned money.

4. Paying your bills before you pay yourself. It's a terrible and lazy habit. If you decide to save

$20 from every paycheck but wait until all your bills are paid first, you will find, invariably, that the $20 never gets saved.

5. Loading up the credit card. Yes, you know there's a limit and you're going to keep spending until you get pushback.

6. Eating lunch out every day. A surefire way to expand expenses.

7. Having every conceivable channel on your cable system, Netflix, and every possible mode of entertainment, mostly because the package looks like the "best deal" or the incremental cost between package 1 and package 2 is very small.

8. Qualifying for your company's 401(k) match and not taking advantage of free money.

9. Having discretionary spending that exceeds your fixed costs.

10. Traveling at peak times rather than waiting to take advantage of off-peak and saving the difference.

11. Free-for-all spending.

12. Not placing limits on gifts. This is a huge issue, especially at holiday time, and then January becomes a month of grief and panic.

13. Neglecting to consider the tax implications of your transactions (i.e., short- vs. long-term capital gains).

14. Paying penalties rather than making the effort to pay quarterly estimated taxes where appropriate.

15. Carrying balances on your credit cards each month.

16. Paying ATM fees because going to a free machine is inconvenient.

17. Renewing magazines and other subscriptions even if you haven't picked up a volume in months.

18. Renewing your insurance policies without considering whether you still need the coverage or maintaining low deductibles when you can afford a greater level of self-insurance.

19. Not actively saving for specific goals.

20. Having no idea what you spend each year by line item. If you don't have a pretty good idea of how much you spend, it's a problem.

21. Having "no" as the driver in your decision-making. Delayed gratification is missing from your vocabulary.

In fact, if you struggle with money, money decisions, and focusing on your values, you can rest assured that your "autopilot" has been engaged and is in control of the vehicle. The problem with your autopilot is that it is hardwired to make the easy, least painful, and most "now"-oriented decisions, even if the end result is crash and burn. That's what happens when we disconnect from the decisions that make a difference in our overall achievement of our dreams. It is a further example of deflecting responsibility to some unnamed, masked entity who in controlling the train. Way back in the 1970s there was a young comedian named Flip Wilson. One of his most loveable characters was the outlandish Geraldine, who, when asked to defend why she did something, answered, "The devil made me do it!" It worked for Geraldine, but unless you are a member of the Linda Blair fan club, the responsibility lies in your hands, in your mind, and on your lips.

Making the Effort to Take Control

Creating new habits is hard work. But it is joyful change. Powerful! Life-giving! Though it sounds like really big stuff, it is actually a gift of loving yourself enough to make changes that bring you closer to your life's purpose. You have to believe that is true in order for you to gain the momentum of change. Consider this: Remaining in a state of action or inaction that leads you to misery and chaos is not an act of love. Quite the opposite. The decision to shift your thinking and your actions is the act of ultimate love for yourself and your loved ones. If achieving financial security is important rather than winding up depending on your children for support or government assistance, then the active choices you make now are vital.

Ask yourself whether you deserve happiness, comfort, and security. If the answer is no, I recommend that you take that up with a qualified professional who can help you examine these feelings and beliefs. It's hard work, but certainly better than living your life under the burden of this terrible cloud. If you do believe that you deserve to achieve peace and comfort in your money life, then let that be your mantra, morning, noon, and night and a reason to make the changes necessary to free yourself from living your life on autopilot.

As you emerge from the clouds into the blue skies of self-control, expect turbulence. Feelings of failure, remorse, exasperation, and being overwhelmed are normal. Your ability to make small, sustainable changes leads you from failure to success. For example, if spending is a problem, leave the credit card home. If you're an online shopper, do not leave your credit card stored by the Website where you normally shop. This way you are forced to get up, get your wallet, and enter your information. The more convenient it is to effectuate the "autopilot"/"autopurchase" the harder is it to sustain change. Another way to interrupt your pattern is to stop and ask *why* this is important and necessary. (Hint: *Because* is not an acceptable answer.)

Change is difficult for almost everyone, so don't think that you're the only one. This is where having an accountability/support partner is really helpful, and you can put in place a checks and balance system. For example, you can each decide that all expenditures not in the budget need to be discussed before a purchase. You can also impose a 24-hour hold before you buy anything. Anything that will break the autopilot habits and replace them with a mindful and considered process will move you ever closer to living richly.

Changing habits requires crystal-clear purpose and a well-thought-out support system. Go on—reach over and turn off the autopilot. You now have the controls and the ability to live intentionally and richly.

Where to Go from Here

The idea of the Feel Rich Project is to offer a better way to define what it means to live richly and feel that your success is defined by *your* values and no one else's.

The previous 11 chapters have taken you through an examination of your past and present, and have prepared you for your preferred future. My hope is that you will use the great work you've done and re-read it over and over. Making shifts in your life is not a "one and done" endeavor.

Instead of focusing on what choices you have made that entailed hard decisions, keep your attention firmly on those *musts*. When you put it in such stark terms, such as "I am willing to give up _____ in order to be debt-free, or live a financially secure life," the pain isn't so bad. Remember: Whatever obstacles you've faced probably didn't happen without your involvement. Your decisions were somehow involved.

Tie a secure connection between your values (what you define as true wealth) and your actions. If you are in alignment, you will generally make the right decisions to support your most important goals.

Many of us confuse needs and wants. It's just the child part of us. It doesn't make us bad; it's just how we were wired. Guilt, shame, and jealousy need to be replaced with gratitude, self-love, and valuation for the gifts we possess and our desire to live a more values-based life. Remember the stories that illustrate both broken messages and values-oriented beliefs. Call it the "warning and the hope," a place to run from and a place to work toward.

The most reasonable and successful approach is to create a rational plan of incremental shifts. Your comfort zone, if you are mired in destructive habits, is the place you need to leave. Bumping up against your comfort zone is sure to lead to doubt and fear, but if your reason to change the status quo is strong enough, you will, little by little, expand your zone and grow into new and exciting abilities. Just as weight loss is achived one ounce at a time (barring radical surgery), changes in your money life come one small decision at a time.

In examining your current money reality, you have dissected your financial picture. You have created a better understanding of where your money goes, how much of your spending is fixed, and how much you can control. This knowledge is necessary in making decisions. Once you have attained this information, your job is to monitor, monitor, monitor—checking your progress and taking action where appropriate.

You have done important work in these chapters. There are challenges and obstacles, and things that you cannot control. For those unexpected occurrences, your ability to activate your resilience is a powerful tool. You have proven your resilience time and again with every small change, every incremental step, every decision that brings you closer to living your dreams.

Remember: Only you can define what makes you feel rich. Only you can alter broken, destructive beliefs and replace them with healthy, supportive ones. What you value most highly is your richness and success. It's not about "stuff"; it's about those you love and the security and comfort of knowing that you are moving toward—and not away from—your life's riches.

INDEX

ABOUT THE AUTHOR

Michael F. Kay, CFP® is president of Financial Life Focus, a fee-only multi-advisor financial life planning firm and the author of *The Business of Life*. He and his financial advice have been featured in *The New York Times*, *The Wall Street Journal*, *Fox Business*, *Forbes* and *Psychology Today*. Through his books, workshops, speeches, and client base, he's helped thousands of women, men, and families master their financial lives. He is a former trumpet player and lives in West Orange, New Jersey.

http://michaelfkay.com/